SOCIOLOGY IN FOCUS SERIES
General Editor: Murray Morison

Crime

Ian Marsh

Lecturer in Sociology,
North East Wales Institute of Higher Education

LONGMAN
London and New York

LONGMAN GROUP LIMITED
*Longman House, Burnt Mill, Harlow, Essex CM20 2JE, UK
and Associated Companies throughout the World.*

Published in the United States of America
by Longman Inc., New York

*First published 1986
Second impression 1987
ISBN 0 582 35562 1*

Set in 10/11pt Bembo, Linotron 202

*Produced by Longman Singapore Publishers Pte Ltd
Printed in Singapore*

British Library Cataloguing in Publication Data

Marsh, Ian
    Crime — (Sociology in focus)
    1. Crime and criminals — Great Britain
    I. Title   II. Series
    364'.941   HV6947

ISBN 0-582-35562-1

Library of Congress Cataloging-in-Publication Data

Marsh, Ian.
    Crime.

    (Sociology in focus series)
    Bibliography: p.
    Includes index.
    1. Crime and criminals. 2. Crime and criminals —
    Great Britain.   I. Title.   II. Series.
    HV6025.M338 1986   364'.941   85–23854
    ISBN 0–582–35562–1

Contents

Acknowledgements

We are grateful to the following for permission to reproduce copyright material:

George Allen & Unwin for extracts from pp 130–131, 142–144 *Cheats at Work: An Anthropology of Workplace Crime* by G Mars (1982); Macmillan, London and Basingstoke for extracts from pp 128–130 *Schooling the Smash Street Kids* by P Corrigan (1979) and pp 7–8, 213–215 *Hooligan: A History of Respectable Fears* by G Pearson (1983).

Series introduction

Sociology in Focus aims to provide an up-to-date, coherent coverage of the main topics that arise on an introductory course in sociology. While the intention is to do justice to the intricacy and complexity of current issues in sociology, the style of writing has deliberately been kept simple. This is to ensure that the student coming to these ideas for the first time need not become lost in what can appear initially as jargon.

Each book in the series is designed to show something of the purpose of sociology and the craft of the sociologist. Throughout the different topic areas the interplay of theory, methodology and social policy have been highlighted, so that rather than sociology appearing as an unwieldly collection of facts, the student will be able to grasp something of the process whereby sociological understanding is developed. The format of the books is broadly the same throughout. Part one provides an overview of the topic as a whole. In part two the relevant research is set in the context of the theoretical, methodological and policy issues. The student is encouraged to make his or her own assessment of the various arguments, drawing on the statistical and reference material provided both here and at the end of the book. The final part of the book contains both statistical material and a number of 'Readings'. Questions have been provided in this section to direct students to analyse the materials presented in terms of both theoretical assumptions and methodological approaches. It is intended that this format should enable students to exercise their own sociological imaginations rather than to see sociology as a collection of universally accepted facts, which just have to be learned.

While each book in the series is complete within itself, the similarity of format ensures that the series as a whole provides an integrated and balanced introduction to sociology. It is intended that the text can be used both for individual and classroom study, while the inclusion of the variety of statistical and documentary materials lend themselves to both the preparation of essays and brief seminars.

PART 1

Introduction and overview

1 Introduction

Crime and criminals are topics of endless fascination. A glance at the newspapers or at the television programme schedules provides a clear indication of this enormous interest in crime, both 'real life' crime and fictional crime. Yesterday's public enemies and villains have a habit of becoming present-day cult figures. Stories of the Great Train Robber Ronnie Biggs and his life in Brazil arouse feelings close to affection, for example.

There are a variety of possible reasons for this interest. It may demonstrate a sense of outrage toward the criminal and the enjoyment of seeing the wrongdoer punished and justice being done, given that in the majority of crime stories and programmes the criminals come off worse. It may be that we secretly admire those who attempt to 'beat the system', and that we sympathise with the underdog. Alternately, this interest might demonstrate the excitement and enjoyment gained from reading about and watching that which we ourselves could not or would not do; a sort of substituted excitement.

Whatever the reasons, murder, rape, robbery, large-scale fraud and embezzlement, drug smuggling, gang warware, delinquency and so on make good subjects for conversation and exciting and profitable stories and films. The number of box-office successes at the cinema which have had crime as their central theme illustrates this vast interest – films such as *The Godfather, The French Connection, The Sting, Butch Cassidy, Warriors, Scarface* and many more you could name. Someone from a different culture, or world, visiting our society could be excused for thinking that crime was a basic, ever-present feature of our everyday lives. In reality the majority of people are not involved in such spectacular criminality. However, we do not need to look far to see how the influence and effects of crime have imprinted themselves on our social environment. Locks, security staff, police, prisons, the mass media, insurance cover, safes and so on reflect the extent of crime. There would be little need to employ security guards or insure against theft if crime did not occur.

Before we look at sociological research and theory on crime, it is necessary to define and make clear what our subject matter is. Crime is often equated with the term deviance, but there are problems in using the two terms interchangeably, as substitutes for one another. While crime is frequently a major area of the study of deviance the relationship between the two needs to be made clear.

What is crime?

The definition of crime is fairly clear cut. It is generally accepted that a crime is an act which breaks the criminal law. In addition to breaking the criminal law, a crime can be followed by criminal proceedings, including punishment. The phrase 'can be followed by' indicates that not all crime does actually result in police action and prosecution, an issue we will examine in more detail in a discussion of criminal statistics (Chapter 4).

However, the criminal law is not fixed and static, it varies over time and from area to area. Therefore, the actions which are defined as criminal will vary with different social settings – in different societies and different periods of time. In other words, crime is a *relative concept;* it can only be defined in relation to particular criminal laws which are effective at particular times and in particular societies. Such laws, and the criminal proceedings or punishments that follow the breaking of them, are not constant, they are always liable to change.

No doubt you can think of various acts which are crimes in this country but not in other countries; and of behaviour which is against the criminal law of other societies but which is not criminal in Britain. The clearest illustrations of the relative nature of crime can be seen by comparing distinct and different cultures. Bigamy, for example, is a serious crime in Britain yet it is normal and accepted practice in other countries. Similarly, alcohol drinking is accepted and legal in some countries yet illegal and severely punished in certain Moslem countries. Even countries with broadly similar cultures can differ in what they define as criminal. In certain states of the USA the possession of small quantities of marijuana is not a criminal offence, although it is in Britain.

As well as differing from place to place, what is defined as crime changes over time. In Britain today we have different criminal laws and hence a different range of crime from those which once existed. Homosexuality between consenting adults aged 21 or over, and abortion during a certain period of pregnancy, are not criminal offences at present, although they have been in the past. It is worth bearing in mind, however, that the de-criminalising of an activity (the removing of an activity from the scope of criminal law) does not mean that it necessarily becomes generally accepted. Although homosexuality is no longer against the law, homosexuals still face a good deal of criticism and stigma.

The fact that what is seen as crime varies with different societies does not affect the definition of crime – as an act which breaks the criminal law of the particular society. Thus, our definition of crime is based on criminal laws which are made by particular governments and enforced by established criminal procedure. Crime, then, has to be seen as a socially variable phenomenon: it reflects what particular societies and governments, at particular times, include within their criminal laws and practices.

Deviance

Deviance is a much wider and more vague concept than is crime, and is therefore less easy to define. The term itself is based on the verb 'to deviate', meaning to stray from, to digress. In one sense, deviance could be taken to mean any behaviour that differs from the normal, any uncommon or unusual behaviour. From such a position, deviant behaviour could be extremely good or herioc behaviour, such as risking one's life to help others or showing courage over and above the line of duty. It could be behaviour that is different or unusual in away that is disapproved of, such as stealing or children-battering. Or, it could be behaviour which is seen as eccentric or bizarre, such as not wearing shoes and socks in conventional situations or carrying on prolonged conversations with the plants in one's garden.

However, in sociology and in everyday use, the term deviance is generally applied to situations where the behaviour is disapproved of and subject to some form of punishment. Deviance is thus used to describe behaviour that is outside the rules of society; and these rules can be legal rules or social and moral rules, rules about the conventional way to dress or to speak to other people, for example. Also, deviant behaviour is behaviour that can result in some form of punishment; and this punishment can be either a formal, legal punishment or take the form of social and moral disapproval. Deviance is behaviour which does not follow the expectations or norms of the majority in society, and it leads to a hostile and critical reaction from the majority. It is this social reaction which generates and defines deviance. In other words, for an action to be deviant it has to cause some form of critical reaction and disapproval from others in the particular society. No action is deviant in itself: it has to excite some reaction from others.

In defining and distinguishing crime and deviance we have referred to rules, laws and norms, and to behaviour which does not follow them. They are terms which you will encounter in the study of crime and deviance and it might be helpful to define and discuss each at this stage.

Rules, laws and norms

A rule is a common and widely used term. Rules can be formal and written or they can be unwritten. The rules of a factory may be written down and serve as strict regulators of behaviour. In contrast, the rules of dress or of how we eat are unwritten guides to behaviour. In all cases, however, a rule is something that is held and accepted as right and legitimate by the members of a group or society.

Laws are perhaps the best example of written, formal rules. There are specific penalties drawn up to punish those who break laws. Generally speaking, the most important rules in society are those that make up the law, with laws decided upon by powerful and influential groups in society. In order to ensure that everyone keeps to the laws there are specific penalties, such as fines or imprisonment, for those found guilty of breaking the law. Unlike other rules, such as rules of dress or of grammar, laws can always be enforced by law enforcement agencies such as the police and the courts in the last resort.

We have defined crime as behaviour which breaks the criminal law. However, there are different categories of law, with criminal law being one such category. There is a basic distinction in the laws of this country between the criminal and the civil law. Broadly, civil law refers to the resolving of disputes between individuals, and the breaking of civil law results in less severe penalties, often the paying of compensation or 'damages'.

A norm is very much a general term, it is an expected standard of behaviour shared by members of a social group. Norms can be thought of as unwritten rules. Any group of people will, over time, develop common rules governing their behaviour, and these rules are often described as norms. Examples of these unwritten rules are that parents should play with their children, or that one should respond in the appropriate manner to a 'good morning' greeting. Norms are, therefore, ideal standards of behaviour. They are part of the culture of society and are passed on from one generation to the next. Although many norms are shared by the majority in society, there are also intra-group norms which govern the behaviour of particular groups of people but which may not be accepted by the majority. In a school, teachers may share different norms to students, and different groups of students (and teachers) may share different norms.

The relationship between crime and deviance

We have defined crime as an act which breaks the criminal law and deviance as behaviour which breaks or departs from the norms or standards of the majority in society. From these definitions you will see that crime and delinquency are one form of deviance (strictly speaking, delinquency refers to anti-social and illegal behaviour, but in sociology it is usually linked with 'juvenile' and used to refer to the criminality and misconduct of youths). They are perhaps the most obvious form of deviance, in that crime is clearly behaviour which breaks the standards of society and which can result in some punishment. It should also be apparent, though, that there is a variety of other behaviour which is outside the rules and standards of society but which does not break the criminal law. Being an alcoholic is not against the law, and not criminal, although it is deviant. Similarly, becoming a hermit and avoiding contact with other people would be considered deviant behaviour but it is not criminal. Without labouring the point, it is clear that not all deviant behaviour is criminal, and it is important to be aware of the distinction between the two concepts.

Thus, deviance is a broader concept than crime. However, and to complicate the issue, it does not necessarily follow that all crime is always viewed as deviant. You might be able to think of crimes that are not generally regarded as deviant – crime committed in self-defence, for example. Although theft is illegal it is often regarded as normal and acceptable practice when an individual 'borrows' materials from his or her place of work for personal use – such as stationery, or makes 'phone calls on an office telephone. Thus the distinction between crime and deviance is by no means straightforward and the relationship between the two has often been poorly understood. In this study we shall be examining crime, and while deviance does overlap with crime it is important not to simply identify crime with deviance.

The study of crime

In the sociological study of crime, as with other areas of sociological study, the student is faced with an ever growing body of research and argument. But there is a general agreement on the major works which form the bases of the different perspectives or theories; as with other subjects, sociology has its 'classics'. Chapter 2 of this book covers the major theoretical approaches. It includes much that is central to the accepted body of the sociology of crime and deviance, but aims to introduce this material in an easily accessible form. In Chapter 3 we will look at specific examples of criminal behaviour, and will discuss and criticise some of the common assumptions about the nature and extent of crime in contemporary society. We will examine the history of delinquency in an attempt to correct the notion, or perhaps myth, that such behaviour is a uniquely modern phenomenon that indicates a degeneration of standards of behaviour in present-day society. We will investigate the widely held belief that crime is a working-class phenomenon through an examination of some predominantly middle-class crimes, in particular business or corporate crime. Similarly, we will look at female crime and the reasons why this makes up such a small proportion of known criminality.

Part Three is divided into two chapters. The first, Chapter 4, deals with the measurements of crime, the extent and character of recorded crime and the dangers of assuming that the criminal statistics accurately reflect the amount and character of crime that does occur. Chapter 5, includes extended readings from a range of studies in the sociology of crime. Most of the readings will be from studies cited in the previous chapters, although some will be from studies not cited in the main text. This chapter will enable students to read and appreciate original sociological writing and research, rather then rely on reviews provided in textbooks.

Before we commence with these main themes, some general comments on the sociology of crime as it is, and has been, studied might help students to appreciate the theories and research discussed in what follows. Sociology is a relatively new discipline or subject, although the issues examined by sociologists and the explanations put forward have a much longer history. Crime has persistently interested and worried people, and attempts to make sense of crime and criminal behaviour have appeared in literary and intellectual writings throughout the ages.

The world of crime and, therefore, the sociological study of crime is vast and uncertain. There is a massive amount of crime which is never recognised. The need for criminals to be secretive and not to advertise themselves adds to this uncertainty, and makes the study of crime more problematic than many other areas of sociological study. Naturally enough, those who commit crimes will tend to conceal their actions and protect themselves. The usual aim of the criminal is to remain anonymous, particularly if he or she wishes to continue to engage in criminal actions.

The secretive nature of crime raises a number of problems for the study of crime. In the first instance, there is a need to be alert to the potential for, and presence of, crime in conventional and ordinary settings. Widespread and systematic crime occurs in normal, everyday situations. A study of a bakery in south-east England uncovered a highly organised system of stealing from work and of fiddling of customers by the bread salesmen (Ditton, 1977). In a similar manner, various other studies have indicated that a wide and diverse range of crime occurs at the workplace. Clearly, crime is not a rare occurrence, but it is hidden methodically, and this raises problems for research.

Initially it is necessary to find the subjects for study. How does one locate a fraud expert, for example? Then, once located, the subjects have to be convinced that they can safely discuss their criminal behaviour. The process of gaining the confidence of criminals is liable to be time-consuming and thus expensive. Research into crime is likely to take comparatively longer than into other areas of social behaviour. Months or years may pass before intimacy and trust develop, and before a reasonable range of criminal actions can be observed closely.

Research and study problems are not limited to the area of crime and criminals. However, the effective study of crime requires the development of intimate associations with people who are by nature suspicious and unwilling to talk to outsiders. Bearing these problems and points in mind, the participant observation method of research has been particularly effective in the study of crime. Participant observations involves the observing of a phenomenon as an 'insider', through contacting and gaining acceptance from the people or groups being studied. While other research methods, such as interviews or questionnaires, can be effectively used to gain a wider picture, participant observation enables the investigator to understand behaviour through direct, personal experience. This is not to suggest that such observation is itself a straightforward method of investigation. The researcher has to remain an objective and outside recorder of events at the same time as being closely involved with the people and events that are being studied. Furthermore, it is difficult for the participant observer not to exert some influence on the events that are being observed. Some of the problems inherent in the sociological study of crime are illustrated in the first reading in Chapter 5 (pages 76–77).

In what follows we will introduce various aspects of the sociological study of crime, and examine theories and measurement of crime, and illustrations of specific criminal behaviour.

However, it is important to bear in mind that while most people break some, if not many, of the laws of their society, few people are found guilty of criminal offences. It is useful, therefore, to ask initially why so many people do not become recognised as criminals: to look at why so many conform, or at least do not become regular or serious offenders against the criminal law.

In exploring this problem, it is common to point to two basic types of social control or restraint. The *informal* mechanisms of control, which centre around the socialisation process – people learn that stealing, cheating and the like are wrong; and the *formal* mechanics, which involve formal, legally established penalties. In analysing and explaining crime we will need to examine why these control mechanisms do not exert the same influence on all individuals and social groups.

Discussion exercise

To elaborate on this division and to gain a clearer understanding of the different types of social control, it would be useful for you to try a brief exercise, answering and discussing the following questions. These questions could be looked at within small groups of students.

1 Ask yourself and your colleagues why you follow the laws of society.

   Do the answers given suggest that laws are followed because they are agreed with and felt to be right – indicating the influence of informal control mechanisms? Or do they suggest that laws are followed because of the fear of being caught and punished – indicating the influence of formal control mechanisms?

2 Why do you not steal from shops? (Assuming that you don't!)

   Is it because you believe it wrong to do so, or because you are afraid of being caught and of the consequences if you are? In other words, are formal or informal mechanisms of control the major influence?

   Alternatively, if you do steal from shops what would stop you doing so? Better security and greater risk? Or, becoming convinced that such actions are wrong?

3 Would you steal from shops if it could be guaranteed that you would not get caught?

'Yes' answers to this question would suggest that formal social control mechanisms are the major influence with regard to shoplifting.

4 Would you distinguish between different types of shop? Between a small, local shop where there it likely to be less security, and a large supermarket or department store?

Of course, it is not always easy to pinpoint exactly why we do or do not engage in a particular action. Often the reasons will reflect a mixture of informal and formal social controls, while the importance of either will vary with different circumstances. Although it might be very easy to steal from a friend or colleague and not get caught most people would feel this to be 'wrong', yet such feelings may not exert such a strong influence over decisions as to whether to steal from a larger and less personal victim.

PART 2

Sociology and crime

2 Explaining crime: theories of criminality

Most people have their own notions or theories as to what causes criminal behaviour. For example, lack of discipline in the home, genetic defects, poverty, mixing with the 'wrong sort' have all been proposed as causes of criminality. While such notions may all contains some elements of truth, they are by no means complete explanations of criminal behaviour. This chapter will examine a range of theories which attempt to explain such behaviour. Although the major theoretical explanations are covered in the numerous introductions to the sociology of crime and deviance and to sociology generally, some review of these theories is necessary before embarking upon an examination of specific, substantive examples of criminal behaviour. As this is not a book on criminological theories, what follows will be a brief overview of a wide range of theories and explanations.

First, a word of warning might be in order. It would be naive to expect to uncover any ultimate explanation or basic cause for criminal behaviour, given the extensive and diverse behaviour that is encompassed by the term crime. Suppose, for example, that it could be proved that one cause of delinquency was lack of parental supervision. It might still be necessary to ask why delinquency occurred with one son or daughter but not another. Also, there would be the further question of why the parents had not provided adequate supervision. Perhaps this was because of their poor living conditions which would raise the question of why they were in poor housing. Was this because of governmental housing policy or a poor employment record on the part of the bread-winner of the family? Clearly, we are getting further and further away from the causes of delinquent behaviour, and it is perhaps wisest to think in terms of causal processes when looking at criminal behaviour.

Biological and psychological theories

Before examining the major sociological pespectives on crime, it is useful to refer to theories from outside of sociology, from other academic disciplines. Thus, we will look initially at biological and psychological theories.

Biological theories

Biological (or physiological) explanations are based on the notion that some individuals are predisposed to criminal behaviour because of their genetic make-up. The individual criminal is born so; and this is usually put down to 'faulty chromosome patterns', or, more vaguely, to 'hereditary traits'.

The most famous exponent of this approach was the nineteenth-century Italian physician, **Cesare Lombroso**. In his book *L'Uomo Delinquente*, Lombroso developed a complex description of what he called the 'born criminal', who could be recognised by a variety of physical characteristics, in particular facial characteristics – for example large jaws and ears, and high cheek bones. In the medical faculty at the University of Rome there is a gallery of portraits of splendidly ugly delinquents who were used to illustrate Lombroso's theory. To use his own language:

> Thus were explained anatomically the enormous jaws, high cheek bones, prominent superciliary arches, solitary lines on the palms, extreme size of the orbits, handle-shaped or sessile ears found in criminals, savages and apes, insensibility of pain, extremely acute sight, tattooing, excessive idleness, love of orgies and the irresistible craving for evil for its own sake. . .

These explanations see the delinquent individual as inherently more prone to criminal behaviour than the non-delinquent. They have been widely criticised and rejected by sociologists. Lombroso's work, for example, was based on his examination of people in prison in Italy. This would, necessarily, ignore the fact that many criminals do not go to prison, and that, perhaps, people in prison are not always criminal.

Most advocates of biological theories do not express themselves in the same bizarre language and style as Lombroso, and such theories of crime are not merely historical relics that died with Lombroso. In a major study of institutionalised delinquents (delinquents in some form of custody) in the USA in the 1950s, **Sheldon and Eleanor Glueck** found that delinquent boys were twice as likely to have a mesomorphic build, a chunky, muscular phsique, compared with non-delinquent boys. However, the fact that the study was restricted to institutionalised delinquents limits the validity of the association between body build and crime and delinquency. It may be that tougher-looking delinquents are more liable to be put away than fragile looking ones. Furthermore, it has been found that the association between delinquency on the one hand and height, weight and physique on the other is greatly reduced once social, background factors are taken into account. For example, lower working-class people are more likely to be mesomorphic as a result of their diet and continual manual labour, and this class grouping is more likely to be found represented in the criminal statistics.

With regard to the links between criminal behaviour and inherited characteristics, there have been a number of theoretical explanations suggesting an association between criminality and particular personality characteristics. An example of this more sophisticated biological approach is the work of Hans Eysenck, who has argued in a series of studies, that there is a link between genetically based personality characteristics and criminal behaviour. He maintains that there is a link between characteristics such as extroversion and criminal behaviour. An individual's degree of extroversion or introversion is inherited, determined by his or her genetic make-up. The link with crime found by **Eysenck** was that when prisoners were tested for extroversion, more extroverts were found than in the general population. Eysenck then argues that extroversion is the inherited basis of criminal behaviour. Extroverts take longer to learn the rules of society, they are more likely to break them, and thus more likely become convicted criminals.

As with Lombroso's work and the Gluecks' study discussed above, by starting with institutionalised criminals, it is assumed that all prisoners are criminals and that most criminals do, in fact, go to prison. The people who get caught and imprisoned may not be a representative picture of all criminals.

The major problem faced by theories suggesting a link between genetic make-up and criminal behaviour is the difficulty of distinguishing between genetic and environmental effects. While some genetic influence cannot be ruled out, just what is inherited remains very unclear.

Psychological theories

These theories share certain similarities with biological explanations. They stress the link between criminal behaviour and specific personality traits or characteristics. Psychological theories, however, see these characteristics as a result of unusual or abnormal experiences, rather than as inherited. Thus, as with biological theories, crime is seen as pathological (a disease), as something to be looked at from the medical point of view. However, psychological causes are seen as treatable, whereas biological causes mark the individual for life. In those cases there is no possible treatment, one is born a criminal.

Many psychological theories refer to faulty parent–child relationships, such as abnormal experiences in early childhood having a lasting effect and influence on personality. Studies in this area have indicated that too strict or too lax parental attitudes increase the risk of delinquency (the work of John Bowlby, for example); they have found that if a young child is deprived of close personal relationships with parents or parent figures then 'problem behaviour' is more common. It is well established that in the delinquent-prone, home discipline is more liable to be too lax, strict or erratic. However, it is patently obvious that parents can be a good or bad influence and example for their children, and this fact can hardly be used to explain present patterns of crime. The majority of offenders do not come from disturbed or broken homes, and many broken homes do not produce delinquents.

Of course, this last point does not show that there is *no* link between parent–child relations and crime and delinquency. The problem with assessing the influence of parental and family dimensions, such as weak supervision or parental criminality, is the fact that they are closely linked to various aspects of social and economic disadvantage, such as poverty, overcrowding and poor housing. And it may be that these disadvantages help to cause parental difficulties, and hamper good parenting.

We can hardly do justice to the wide scope of psychological theories here, but there are some basic ideas and assumptions which underlie such theorizing. These stress the importance of family relationships and upbringing during the early years, and conclude that anti-social, and by implication criminal, behaviour results from faulty personality development.

To summarise, these biological and psychological theories hold that the criminal is a particular type of person, apart from the rest of society and with a special predisposition toward criminal behaviour. They are based on the idea that criminal behaviour is either inherited or a consequence of unique, individual experiences. Before we look at sociological explanations it might be useful to ask yourself, or to discuss with colleagues, whether you feel that criminals are different 'types' of person.

While there are, no doubt, predispositions toward criminal behaviour, and clearly certain characteristics are inherited, most sociologists would reject these 'individual pathology' sort of theories. They lack convincing supporting evidence. While some offenders suffer from mental disorders the vast majority do not. Furthermore, if criminals are abnormal then it follows that a large proportion of the population must also be abnormal. For numerous studies have shown that a high percentage of the population have committed criminal offences, in particular high proportions of juveniles, and it is difficult to believe that they are all different or abnormal.

Sociological theories

We said above that sociologists would reject non-sociological explanations of crime. This is not because such explanations are 'wrong', but because they are incomplete or inadequate. In Chapter One, it was stressed that crime cannot be considered aside from its social context, that it is dependent on society defining certain actions as criminal, and on the reaction of others to such actions. Thus, we have to see crime and the criminal in relation to the social structure, to specific social conditions and opportunities. While sociological explanations vary considerably in their emphasis on the different factors within the social structure which can be linked with crime, there is a general acceptance of social forces as causing or influencing criminal behaviour.

In our discussion of sociological explanations we will concentrate on the three major sociological perspectives and how they analyse and interpret crime – Functionalism, Interactionism and Marxism. However, these perspectives are broad schools of thought and include often distinct strands of theorising. Also, by no means all sociological theories of crime fit neatly into one or other 'ism', but often straddle different perspectives. Nonetheless, following these conventional divisions does enable us to discuss sociological theories of crime as they have developed. It enables different theories to be understood in a historical, chronological sequence, one set of theories developing from and often criticising previous work. Thus, the whole of this section will read something like a 'debate'. At the risk of oversimplification, functionalist approaches were challenged by interactionist sociology in the 1960s and 1970s; which has itself been criticised by the revival of Marxist-based theories.

Functionalist theories

Functionalist theory is not just one overall explanation or interpretation, and the examples we will look at have quite distinct emphases. The general, underlying characteristic common to all functionalist-based theory is a stress on the importance of shared norms and values which form the basis for social order. Crime consists of acts which break or depart from these shared norms and values.

CLASSIC FUNCTIONALIST THEORY: EMILE DURKHEIM

Classic functionalist theory points to the function of crime for society, and suggests that crime is universal, normal and functional to society; criminal behaviour helps to sustain conformity and stability and is thereby functional. Given that crime is behaviour that breaks rules, it might seem odd that functionalists argue that it is necessary and useful for society. However, while agreeing that crime must be controlled, this functionalist argument is that some criminal behaviour has positive and useful functions.

This approach or argument is based on the work of **Emile Durkheim,** the founding father of functionalist sociology.

Durkheim saw crime as a normal phenomenon in society: 'it is a factor in public health and an integral part of all societies. . . crime, is, then, necessary' (from *The Rules of Sociological Method*, first published in 1895). The fact that some individuals commit acts which break the rules of society is accompanied by a sense of outrage with reinforces, in the majority, support of the rules (both moral and legal) of the society. The presence of the criminal allows the rest to draw together and reaffirm their values. Thus, through opposition to criminal behaviour the social group or society is strengthened.

It is not of course the criminal acts themselves which draw the majority together, but the publicising and punishing of crime, with the public trial of law-breakers also helping to clarify the boundaries of socially acceptable behaviour. Durkheim regards the criminal as someone who provides the community with an opportunity to reassert standards, which he or she had broken or opposed.

It is this argument which leads Durkheim to state that crime is essential to the continuation of society. If society is to exist as a unity there must be an agreement on shared values. For this agreement to exist people need to be able to react against those who depart from or break shared values. It is crime which serves to create this reaction. If societies 'need' crime then it is logical to assume that they will ensure that there will be crime. It is possible for us to imagine a society of saints in which no one committed what we see as crimes, in which everyone behaved in an impeccable manner. However, within such a community, Durkheim argues that the division between what is acceptable and unacceptable behaviour would still exist. Faults which we might see as trivial would create the same scandal and outrage as criminal behaviour does in our society.

Although talking of the inevitability and necessity of crime, Durkheim did not mean to suggest the more crime the better. He saw a certain level of crime as functional from the point of view of social order, but beyond that level it would cease to be functional and become dangerous or pathological. The argument that crime is necessary and functional does not explain the causes of it, nor does it explain why some people are motivated to engage in criminal activities. More recent functionalist work, though, has been concerned with the 'causes' of criminal behaviour.

ROBERT MERTON

Merton starts from the basic functionalist position that social stability is based on a strong consensus of values, which the majority of people come to share. However, not every member of society is in a position to achieve these values. **Merton suggests that criminal and rule-breaking behaviour results from 'differentials in access to the success goals of society by legitimate means'.** What does he mean by this?

In societies where there is a strong emphasis on certain goals, but where the means for obtaining them are unavailable to most citizens, the result is a situation of *anomie*; a situation, in other words, where the rules and standards governing behaviour have lost their influence and force and are liable to be ignored, and where shared norms or rules no longer determine and direct behaviour.

In present-day western society we have cultural goals of material success: plenty of money, a big house, flash cars, pretty girl/handsome boy, for example. Although the desirability of such goals is constantly stressed by society, different groups in society clearly have different degrees of access to them. Certain groups are well equipped to achieve such goals through legitimate means, for example, those with enough wealth and power to transfer to their children. At the other extreme, there are groups who face an enormous task in realising their goals. It is in these circumstances that there occurs, according to Merton, a situation of anomie, with people striving for goals of material success, but not having the opportunities to reach them through legitimate means.

For Merton, such behaviour occurs as a result of a discrepancy or contradiction between the aspirations which society has socialised into its members (the ends or goals) and the way that is provided for the realisation of such aspirations (the means). So people have to devise ways of adapting to this gap between what they want and expect from society and the means they have available to obtain these things. Merton put forward five possible ways of adapting to this gap. Firstly, *conformity*, accepting the goals and means. Secondly, *innovation*, which involves the adoption of unconventional methods of chasing the goals, such as through crime. Thirdly, *ritualism*, abandoning the goals but sticking rigidly to the legitimate means of achieving them. Fourthly, *retreatism*, abandoning both the goals and the means, such as 'dropping out' of society. Fifthly, *rebellion*, giving up the conventional goals and means and replacing them with new ones.

Merton's model or theory does not adequately explain all types of criminal behaviour. It is difficult to point to the material goals which football hooligans or juvenile delinquents are chasing. The theory seems to have a middle class bias in that it assumes that all criminal and rule-breakers accept and cherish middle-class goals, but many delinquent activities do not appear to be aiming for material gains. This is a general danger or problem with theories that are based on a consensus view of society – a view that society is held together by common values, shared by all.

Merton's theory does not explain why some individuals faced with a situation of anomie conform while others break the rules. Nor does it explain why one type of adaptation rather than another occurs; for example, why innovation occurs rather than retreatism, or vice-versa. Also, no explanation is offered as to how society defines criminal behaviour, why some acts are made illegal and others not.

Nonetheless, the work of Merton has certain strengths. It explains criminal behaviour in terms of the structure and culture of society, rather than individual characteristics. Hence it is a *structural theory of crime*. Further, in developing this approach Merton laid the ground for later work on crime based on the notion of *subculture*, the notion that there are certain groups who will be more liable to break the rules of society. We will now review some of the major developments from functionalist theory based on notions of culture and subculture.

Albert Cohen and subcultural theories

In his widely cited study *Delinquent Boys*, Cohen questions whether delinquent behaviour is caused directly by the desire for material goals. While some forms of delinquent behaviour are clearly centred on acquiring goods or money, a large amount of delinquency is expressive in character. That is, it is not directly concerned with material gain; delinquency centering on vandalism or violence is an obvious example.

Cohen looks to the educational system for his explanation of delinquency. Schools, he argues emphasise and embody middle-class values. Thus, individuals socialised into the working classes will suffer from *status frustration*, and will adopt an outlook set on turning the middle-class value system on its head. Anything which the school sees as wrong, the working-class delinquent will see as good; delinquency is explained as a direct denial of middle-class values. In his study, Cohen compares what he terms the 'street corner boy' with the 'college boy'. Because working-class boys suffer disadvantages in the educational system and are not brought up to accept the values of this system, they are likely to reject the school values and form a *delinquent subculture* (Cohen's definition of this subculture is reproduced as Reading 2 in Chapter 5).

Cohen stresses therefore, the collective reponse as central to delinquency, rather than seeing such behaviour as an individual response to the failure to achieve middle-class goals, as Merton argued. His theory is, however, open to similar criticisms to those made about Merton's work. The claim that status frustration is the motivating factor also suffers from a middle-class bias, in that it is assumed that delinquents cherish middle-class status goals, such as educational success. Moreover, it is perhaps doubtful whether many delinquents hold openly oppositional views or values as Cohen suggests. Furthermore, although delinquency is invariably a group activity it does not always take place within organised delinquent gangs, which is the basis of Cohen's theoretical approach. Certainly, organised, structured delinquent gangs do not appear to be the norm in Britain today.

Another 'subcultural'-type theory that stresses deprivation and develops and draws on the work of Merton and Cohen is that of **Cloward and Ohlin**. Briefly, Cloward and Ohlin argue that there is greater pressure on members of the working class to behave criminally or delinquently due to the fact that they have less opportunity to succeed by legitimate means. They agree with Cohen's argument that working-class boys are likely to form and join delinquent subcultures, but they feel he has not taken account of the different and specialised types of subculture that exist. They suggest that the potentially delinquent individual may respond to his situation by joining one of three types of subculture: a criminal subculture, where delinquency is linked with adult criminality; a conflict subculture, which occurs in areas where links between juvenile and adult criminality are not established; and, thirdly, a retreatist or 'escapist' subculture.

Recent developments in the sociology of crime: the deviant as normal

The theories looked at thus far have moved away from the view of the criminal as clearly distinguishable from the non-criminal. The biological and psychological theories stressed this distinctiveness. The functionalist approaches see crime as a reponse of people to their social situation. However, in responding to their situation criminals are seen as becoming distinct from the mainstream, non-criminal population. We will now turn to theoretical approaches which see the criminal as 'normal', and which centre on how society defines certain individuals as criminal or deviant. In particular, the Interactionist and Marxist approaches.

Interactionist theories

To overcome some of the problems associated with the structural and subcultural-orientated theories based on the functionalist perspective, Interactionism has adopted a different theoretical perspective for examining crime and rule-breaking.

One of the major criticisms of these previous theories has been that they have tended to see their subject matter (that is, rule-breaking) as straightforward and easily identifiable – crime being behaviour that breaks certain of the rules of society. This implies that social groups are characterised by consensus. Interactionists would question that implication, and argue that they are made up of a plurality of values and norms, which may often conflict. As suggested above, Interactionists would also deny that criminals are essentially different from other, so-called 'normal', people. Various studies have demonstrated that very few people have not broken laws, and many people do so frequently without ever having their 'crimes' recorded. Thus, if a majority of people commit criminal actions it becomes somewhat dubious to maintain a distinction between criminal and non-criminal, in terms of personal chacteristics.

LABELLING

Interactionist approaches to crime and deviance have centred around the concept of labelling, with the term *labelling theory* sometimes used to refer to the Interactionist perspective on rule-breaking. From this viewpoint, the criminal is an individual who has been labelled so by society, and this labelling does not apply to all individuals who break laws. As mentioned, many people who break laws are never found out and are thus not labelled as criminals. Interactionism stresses the arbitrariness of this labelling of someone, or of some action, as criminal. It focusses on the interaction between the criminal or deviant and those who define him/her as such.

The classic statement on the labelling perspective is found in the work of **Howard Becker**:

> Social groups create deviance by making rules whose infraction constitutes deviance and by applying those rules to particular people and labelling them as outsiders. From this point of view deviance is not a quality of the act a person commits, but rather a consequence of the application by others of rules and sanctions to an offender. The deviant is the one to whom that label has been successfully applied; deviant behaviour is behaviour that people so label.
>
> Becker, 1963

Labelling, therefore, refers to the process by which individuals and groups classify and categorise social behaviour and other individuals. If a criminal is a person labelled as such, an initial question we must ask is 'Who does the labelling?' And, when we see terms such as 'social problem' or 'criminal', we need to ask 'who defines these terms?', and to be as concerned with the actions and motives of the labellers as those who are labelled.

The reason for this emphasis on the way in which people are labelled is that laws are essentially political products. They reflect the fact that some groups in society can create laws, and can determine what behaviour is seen as criminal. Interactionists stress that definitions of crime reflect the power of groups who have managed to impose their ideas about right and wrong, normality and so on on society. Of course, there are laws to curb the powerful also. However, Interactionists suggest that they are less frequently and vigorously applied. This point leads us on to an examination of the selective nature of law enforcement.

SELECTIVE ENFORCEMENT OF THE LAW

In a study of the administration of juvenile justice in the USA

Cicourel (*The Social organization of Juvenile Justice*, 1976) looked at the actual process of how delinquency and criminality is defined and applied to certain individuals. Without going into his work in any detail, Cicourel found that white, middle-class youths are less liable to be identified by police and probation officers as having committed or being likely to commit a crime. The police are more likely to react toward those groups and individuals whom they see as being prone to commit criminal actions; often labelling such individuals before they actually commit a criminal act. The police, like most people, have stereotypical views as to the 'typical' criminal or delinquent. In the procedures of arresting and charging individuals and in their treatment in court, there are clear differences across the middle/working-class divide; and these serve to reinforce the public's (and the police's) perception that certain groups are inclined to criminality. Cicourel suggests that certain groups are selected, processed and labelled as criminal.

Interactionist approaches to explaining crime imply that for the purpose of studying such behaviour there is a correlation between being regarded as a criminal and in fact becoming one. Sociological study does not aim to discover who is innocent of the charges against them and who is guilty. For our purposes, being found guilty is the same as being guilty. Now, you might feel that there is a significant difference between a murderer or bank robber and someone who has been wrongfully convicted of murder or bank robbery. However, this difference is not likely to have any effect on the way in which the individuals will be treated. The wrongfully convicted prisoner will be treated identically to any other prisoner by prison officers. Furthermore, protesting one's innocence will be seen as the kind of thing that everyone who is convicted does.

Being convicted involves being identified publicly as a criminal, and it is in this context that we can say that being found guilty is the same as being guilty. Thus, being known to be a criminal is the same as being one in terms of treatment. It is for this reason that Interactionists stress that labelling is crucial to understanding criminal behaviour, as the labelling process publicly identifies individuals as guilty of criminal acts.

THE AMPLIFICATION OF CRIMINALITY
Thus far we have examined the process by which individuals

become labelled. One important issue we have not considered is what happens to the individual once he or she is labelled as criminal. In other words, what is the effect of labelling on the individual?

Labelling an individual will tend to mark them out, and knowing a person has been labelled is liable to influence others' behaviour toward that person. For example, knowing someone has been convicted of theft might influence one's reactions and attitudes to that person. Furthermore, the individual who has been labelled is likely to view him/herself in terms of the label and act accordingly. This leads to a process of *amplification* or snowballing: individuals who are caught and labelled as criminal see themselves so and act accordingly, thus the label becomes more widely applied and firmly fixed, and the criminal becomes more attached to that label. Interactionists argue that societal reaction, in terms of labelling, can actually increase or 'amplify' the criminal behaviour of the labelled individual or group.

This amplification process occurs on the wider, societal level as well as on the individual level. **Jock Young's** work on 'Hippies' and police in London during the late 1960s illustrates this wider application (Young, in Cohen, S. ed., 1971). Young found that the harder the police tried to stamp out drug use the more it grew, becoming a symbol of defiance for hippies. He suggested that the police acted as amplifiers of this illegal behaviour. Attemps to control drug use, through the formation of drug squads, helped to amplify it. The drug squads discovered more cases of drug use, which led to more police manpower and money being invested, which led to more discovery. There was thus a 'spiral of amplification'.

The Interactionist approach – critical comments

Labelling theory implies that criminals are powerless, passive victims who have had the misfortune to be labelled criminal, and have not been able to do anything about it. By placing such emphasis on social reaction it can be argued that Interactionists have minimised the role of the individual criminal. Linked with this point, labelling theories tend to disregard the origins of criminal behaviour. They concentrate on the present situation and the reaction of society and show little interest in the criminal's background, although labelling theory does not argue that all that is involved in making someone a criminal is to call them one. Labelling is acknowledged as a complex process involving social norms and values.

So far as the amplification of criminal behaviour is concerned, no explanation is offered as to how and why this process ends. Logically, the social reaction could be expected to grow, as would the individual's criminality, with all law-breakers becoming extreme and committed criminals. While some follow this path, many others conform again, and do not become committed in their ways. People vary in how they respond to labelling; being labelled may deter criminal activity as well as amplify it. Moreover, labels need not be permanent and irreversible.

Finally, Interactionists lay great stress on social reaction without really attempting to explain why some actions are made illegal, without examining who constructs specific laws, and why. Interactionism raises the issue of the relation between power and crime, but does not really answer it. It concentrates on the specific interactions, the 'drama', without investigating the importance of the social system itself. Interactionists look at the police, the courts and the criminals without examining the power underlying the system. To do this would require an analysis of how decision-making and power is distributed in society. This is an area of investigation central to Marxist-based work on crime.

Marxist theories

Marxist-based studies of crime are sometimes referred to under the titles of radical or critical criminology. This work centres on an examination of how crime is related to the power structure of society. We should remember that neither Marx nor Engels, his co-author, proposed a theory of crime; and it has been later social theorists working within a Marxist framework who have developed a Marxist theory of crime.

From a Marxist perspective crime is largely the product of capitalism, and the relatively high rate of crime in capitalist society is an indicator of the contradictions and problems inherent in such a system. Thus, many forms of crime are to be expected under a capitalist system. This is due, in part, to the ability of the powerful to criminalise and stigmatise that which threatens their interests; and to the fact that basic motivations of capitalist societies, such as materialism and self-enrichment, can be pursued both legally and illegally. In relation to crime, perhaps the crucial question for Marxists is not 'Why does crime occur?', but 'Why doesn't it occur more often?'

Crime and the wider Marxist analysis

A Marxist analysis of crime is not easily explainable, and has to be understood in relation to wider aspects of Marxist theory. As Jock Young suggests, 'it is not the criminal nor even the administration of crime, but, in the final analysis, the system itself that must be investigated'.

Marxists hold that there is a basic distinction between the *economic base* of society, which determines the organisation and structure of society, and the *superstructure*, the cultural, legal, religious, political aspects of society. These aspects of the superstructure reflect the economic base. Therefore, the law will reflect the interests of the dominant economic class, and as an instrument of the dominant class the state passes laws which support its interests. The various social control agencies of the state, such as the police and courts, perform in a way that is consistent with the interests of the powerful, and against the interests of other groups, particularly the working classes.

Criminal law is assumed to express and reflect the interests of the ruling class. As evidence for this, Marxists point out that much of the criminal law is about the protection of property. Furthermore, there has been a vast increase in the range of behaviour that has come under the control of the law. In their introduction to *Critical Criminology* (1975), Taylor, Walton and Young point out that old laws have been reactivated and new laws created in order to control and contain an ever widening range of socially problematic behaviour. New laws have been created in this country to regulate industrial dissent and the rights of workers to organise. This extension of the law has created new criminals who do not fit the picture of the 'typical criminal', the young, working-class male. In view of this, Taylor and colleagues argue that criminology needs to centre on theories of rule-making and breaking in relation to the distribution of power in society.

However, power in modern capitalist societies is not just the ability to influence the way people think, and includes the control of knowledge and of ideas. It is from the *dominant ideology* that standards of acceptable, normal behaviour are defined; and it is from this ideology that what constitutes social problems and criminal actions are also defined. A good example of this is the way in which the law, the media and public opinion view supplementary benefit fraud, 'fiddling the dole'. It is commonly assumed that this is widespread and costs enormous sums of money, and that it is a more serious offence than tax-evasion, which in fact costs the exchequer billions of pounds, far in excess of the cost of social security fiddling.

Various Marxist-based studies have aimed to demonstrate how the law reflects economic interests, viewing the legal system as an instrument that supports the interests of the dominant class against threatening or disruptive behaviour. It has also been argued that the legal system enables the powerful to get away with exploiting other people without actually breaking the law. Frank Pearce has argued that organised crime in the USA is dominated by big business; and William Chambliss, in a detailed study of crime in Seattle, Washington, has demonstrated the numerous interconnections between organised crime and the ruling groups in society.

Another important example of the way in which the criminal law reflects ruling-class interests is the way in which the 'crime problem' tends to be equated with working-class crime, often of a very trivial nature, rather than the more important, in terms of money, *white-collar crime*. White-collar crime is crime that is centred around systematic fraud and fiddling by white-collar, middle-class employers and employees. One aspect of this type of criminality, business or corporate crime, will be discussed in some depth in Chapter 3.

A further aspect of the Marxist approach to crime concerns the way in which the law is enforced. It is argued that the law is selectively enforced in the interests of the ruling classes – an issue dealt with more fully in Chapter 4. Very briefly, the basic Marxist argument is that the selective enforcement of the law, by largely ignoring white-collar/business crime, gives the impression that criminals are mainly from the working classes, which serves to direct attention away from 'ruling-class crime'.

The Marxist approach – critical comments

As we have suggested, Marxist approaches to crime are based on the wider Marxist theory of society. Criticism of this approach to crime would, therefore, require a criticism of Marxist theory as a whole. For example, if the predominance of economic interests and power over other areas of society is not accepted, then the Marxist theory of crime would not be accepted. Nonetheless, some specific issues can be raised.

Firstly, it is difficult to argue that every law defining certain actions as criminal is related to supporting the interests of the dominant classes. Many criminal actions appear to offer little threat to the capitalist class system.

A more basic and crucial point is that the logical conclusion of the Marxist approach would be that the introduction of social-ism will lead to a society without crime, where collective interests and responsibilities are all important. Can one be convinced of this? It is certainly the case that crime rates in socialist countries are far less than in the USA and other capitalist societies. However, even if all criminality in western societies could be related to the capitalist system, there is plenty of evidence of both criminal and deviant behaviour in commun-ist societies, such as theft, murder and dissent. It is doubtful that such activities can be interpreted as remnants from pre-communist society, soon to disappear as socialism or commun-ism comes of age.

3 Studying crime: pictures of contemporary criminality

In the previous chapter we looked at crime and criminality in a very broad and general manner. This chapter will provide a more detailed examination of specific aspects of criminality. In Chapter 4 we will examine the statistics on crime. For the purposes of the present discussion we can say that these statistics display a number of clear patterns. Firstly, the statistics show an ever increasing rate of crime and imply, therefore, that much crime is a new, peculiarly modern phenomenon. Secondly, they show that crime is predominately a working-class phenomenon. Thirdly, that it is a male phenomenon. We will examine and discuss each of these patterns in this chapter, and in doing so will aim to look behind the picture of crime and criminals provided by criminal statistics. Extended readings from a number of the studies we look at will be included in Chapter 5.

Crime as a modern phenomenon

This section will take issue with the notion of crime as somehow unique to contemporary society. While no one would deny the existence of horrendous acts of violence and criminality in earlier times, it is a widely held belief that western, advanced societies are becoming more and more criminal. This is reflected in the tendency to look back to a 'golden age' when these societies were thought to be more peaceful and law abiding.

To examine the truth and relevance of these notions, we will look at juvenile delinquency, in particular hooliganism and vandalism. It is this sort of criminal behaviour which is commonly seen as characteristic of (if not central to) mass, urban society. We have all heard the prophets of social and moral decay recalling the days when such 'senseless and mindless' violence did not exist. Our discussion will be divided into two main parts. Firstly, we will look at the history of delinquency and will refer in some detail to **Geoffrey Pearson's** recent study, *Hooligan: A* *history of respectable fears*, and his attempt to locate the supposed 'golden age' of a traditional way of life based on respect for law and order and all forms of authority. Secondly, we will look at modern delinquency, and specifically football hooliganism.

A history of delinquency

In a journey back through the history of crime and delinquency, Pearson shows that for generations Britain has been plagued by the same problems and fears as today. Yet, the myth that Britain has historically been a stable, peaceful and law-abiding nation, and that violence is somehow foreign to the national character, shows little sign of waning. Pearson searches for the period when such a stable, traditional way of life supposedly held sway. He found this 'golden age' was always just over the horizon, one generation further back (see Reading 3, Chapter 5).

The most striking aspect of the history of delinquency is the consistency with which each generation characterises the youth of the day and the way of life of twenty years previously. So let us start with present-day society and compare it with the situation twenty years or so ago, and then compare that generation with its predecessor. Although there are bound to be difficulties in comparing different ages and periods, such as different definitions of crime, different measuring techniques and a lack of adequate records and poor communications in previous times, an impression of the style and extent of crime – and of the popular concern about it – can nevertheless be formed.

Pearson's study starts with present-day attacks on our 'permissive age' by contemporary public figures and 'guardians of morality'. In March 1982 the *Daily Telegraph* suggested that 'we need to consider why the peaceful people of England are changing. . . over the 200 years up to 1945, Britain became so settled in internal peace'. We have warnings of a massive degeneration among the British people which is destroying the nation. Kenneth Oxford, the Chief Constable of Merseyside, prophesies that 'the freedom and way of life we have been accustomed to for so long will vanish'. There are numerous instances of such statements from prominent politicans and public figures alleging that contemporary society is witnessing an unprecedented increase in violence and decline in moral standards. There is a consistent view that Britain's history has been characterised by stability and decency, and that the moderate 'British way of life' is being undermined by the upsurge in delinquency.

Twenty years previously, however, we can find remarkably similar comments. At the Tory Party conference in 1958 there was discussion about 'this sudden increase in crime and brutality which is so foreign to our nature and our country'. The Teddy Boys were arousing similar apocalyptic warnings of the end of British society. Rock and roll was the musical focus of this youth subculture, and the reaction which the Teddy Boys engendered was one of outrage and panic. The press, in particular, printed sensational reports of the happenings at cinemas and concerts featuring rock and roll films and music. An article in the *Evening News* of 1954 suggested that 'Teddy Boys. . . are all of unsound mind in the sense that they are all suffering from a form of psychosis. Apart from the birch or the rope, depending on the gravity of their crimes, what they need is rehabilitation in a psychopathic institution'. This reaction was widespread, off-duty soliders were banned from wearing Teddy Boy suits and Teddy Boys were viewed by the rest of society as 'folk devils'.

Nowadays, when we look back at old photographs and films of the 1950s rock and roll craze, and the Teddy Boys, it is easy to wonder what all the fuss was about. In comparison to groups who have come since then, they look quite straight. If anything, Teds are remembered with a degree of nostalgia and viewed as something quaint. Quite a contrast with the reaction in the mid-1950s illustrated above.

Could it be that pre-war Britain was charaterised by law-abiding youth and stability? The Second World War has been seen by some as a kind of watershed, with the post-war period being morally inferior to the 'full rich back street life and culture of pre-war England'. However, when we look more closely at this period familiar declarations and allegations appear. In the 1930s there was a similar bemoaning of the 'passing of parental authority' and the 'absence of restraint'. The targets of criticism have a common ring – football rowdyism and the increasing crime and disorder. In the 1920s there were fierce street battles in North London between Spurs and Arsenal fans. It is sometimes implied that such incidents, and delinquencies in general, have become more 'serious' or 'violent' over time. The evidence would not seem to back up such suggestions. Crime in the inter-war years was characterised by razor gangs, feuds between armed gangsters, vice rackets and so on.

Moving back to the turn of the century and the pre- First World War period we seem little nearer to finding the traditional way of life based on a 'healthy respect for law and order'. A wide range of popular culture came under severe criticism in the early twentieth century. The music halls, professional football and the noisy presence of working-class people at seaside resorts on bank holidays were all attacked. As ever, youth of the period were compared unfavourably with previous generations. Baden Powell in his *Scouting for Boys*, published in 1908, suggests that professional football was betraying the British traditions of 'fair play' and sportsmanship:

> Thousands of boys and young men, pale, narrow-chested, hunched-up, miserable specimens, smoking endless cigarettes, numbers of them betting, all of them learning to be hysterical as they groan and cheer in panic unison with their neighbours – the worst sound of all being the hysterical scream of laughter that greets any little trip or fall of a player. One wonders whether this can be the same nation which had gained for itself the reputation of being a stolid, pipe-sucking manhood, unmoved by panic or excitement, and reliable in the tightest of places.

Neither does Victorian Britain provide any comparative baseline of a tranquil, law-abiding society. The first 'Hooligans' of the 1890s and the 'Garotters' of the 1860s do little to kindle nostalgia for Victorian city life and culture. In was in the late 1890s that the words 'Hooligan' and 'Hooliganism' were used to describe delinquent youth. There were regular news reports of Hooligan gangs smashing up coffee-stalls and public houses, robbing and assaulting old ladies, attacking foreigners and setting upon policeman in the streets. In line with later youth subcultures and gangs, Hooligans had a distinct style of dress, and a recognisable look. As with so many of the later youth subcultures, there was no doubt an over reaction to Hooligans. Nevertheless, whether correct or not, there was a widely held feeling that hooliganism was a major problem.

Earlier in the Victorian period, in the winter of 1862, panic swept through respectable London over a new variety of crime

called 'garotting', a type of violent robbery that involved chok-
ing the victim. A Victorian parallel with present-day 'mugging'
perhaps. The press reacted in familiar manner, with *The Times*
observing that it was 'becoming unsafe for a man to traverse
certain parts of London at night'.

The possibility that it was industrialisation that destroyed the
stable and peaceful life of pre-industrial Britain does not appear
to hold up either. Certainly, in the mid-nineteenth century it was
widely felt that life in the previous century had been greatly
superior and that the increase in juvenile crime was a blot on this
age. However, writing in 1751 Henry Fielding paints a very
similar picture with his prediction of an imminent slide into
anarchy when the streets of the cities 'will shortly be impassable
without the utmost hazard'. It is difficult to find evidence that
there has been massive deterioration in the morality and behaviour of the common people, in comparison to the pre-
industrial work. From the late seventeenth century there had
been complaints of increasing wickedness, crime and disorder.
The streets of pre-industrial London were very dangerous, and
there was no effective system of street-lighting nor a police force.

Pearson also examines the recurrent nature of different explanations of the criminal question. Time and again a permissive
present is contrasted with the not too distant past. If such
accusations are accepted, we would be forced to conclude that
with each generation crime and disorder increase dramatically.
Looking back over Pearson's historical review, it is hard to
believe that Britain's cities are any more perilous today than
those of pre-industrial times, or when they were frequented by
gangs of Garotters and Hooligans.

This is not to deny, of course, that crime and violence in
contemporary society is an important social reality. However,
the preoccupation with violence and lawlessness is part of a long
and continuous tradition, rather than a new and unique phenomenon. It is well nigh impossible to compare the rate of crime
over extended periods of time (as Reading 10, Chapter 5, taken
from Pearson's study, indicates). What we can say, though, is that
juvenile crime and street violence have been characteristics of
British society over hundreds of years, rather than being indica-
tive of a contemporary moral and social disintegration. This
does not make it any the less disturbing and below we will
discuss contemporary styles of delinquency in greater detail.

Delinquency in contemporary society

Although violence at seaside resorts on bank holidays appears frightening enough when described by the media, various studies have pointed to the ritualistic character of this and other delinquent activity. **Paul Corrigan** suggests that teenagers behave the way they do at the seaside, or at football matches, because they are looking for a memorable experience to balance the boredom of the rest of their lives. However, teenagers do not go out saying to themselves that they are going to smash a couple of telephone boxes or fight another group of teenagers. They will not know what they are going to do, and will probably end up doing nothing. Certainly there is fighting and delinquency at seaside resorts and elsewhere, but if teenagers were seeking real violence then the casualities would be enormous. As Corrigan puts it: 'The kids are not crazy. They don't want to get stabbed. . . or sent away for six months. What they want out of a gang fight is a nice big bruise. . . that they can show around during the week.'

However, whether ritualistic or not, juvenile delinquency is widespread. The issue we will examine is why delinquency is so attractive to some and unappealing to other youth. In particular, we will look at why the delinquent response is attractive to working-class male youth.

In his study of working-class boys in the north-east of England, Corrigan looks at how and why many of these boys get into trouble and engage in delinquent activities. All of the youths studied were in their last year of school, and all were going to leave at the minimum school leaving age (Corrigan, 1979).

The leisure activities of these youths centred on the 'street', the arena where most illegal activity takes place, where most of the fighting and thieving occurs. They made little use of the youth clubs and other leisure facilities, other than as places to meet their mates. As previous research into juvenile delinquency has found, spare time activities are carried out in groups. In virtually every interview in Corrigan's study the immediate response to the question 'What do you do on Saturday night?' was to mention the 'mates'. So, with regard to delinquency, the two important factors would seem to be the street and the group.

The major activity of the youths seemed to be 'doing nothing', and when asked what they did on the street that was the standard reply. Of course, they were doing something, standing around on corners in groups for example, but as far as the boys were concerned nothing memorable seems to happen to them on Saturday night. When asked a question such as 'What do you do?', it is implied that something more should be going on, that standing around on a corner must be a means to an end. However, standing on street corners or walking around is not done with any definite end in mind. Nevertheless, between the general walking around, carrying on and joking things emerged that the youths called 'ideas', and these ideas formed the basis of group actions. The development and carrying out of such ideas is one of the most active parts of the general 'hanging around'. It is these ideas that lead to what is seen as juvenile delinquency. They are born out of boredom, and a good idea must contain the chance of excitement (Reading 4, Chapter 5 is taken from Corrigan's examination of the street based leisure/delinquent activities of these working-class youths).

Another common diversion is getting into a fight, and, again within the context of 'doing nothing' these fights are important and exciting occasions. They are not particularly violent fights and participants are rarely hurt. When asked, 'What sort of fights?', one of the lads replied, 'Well, not real fights, as some of them might be quite matey. . . when you put the boot in, you put the boot in, but we are friendly after, like'.

The youths studied – and you might like to consider the extent to which their experiences and expectations are commonplace – and are aware that in their leisure time they are doing nothing, are bored with it. Essentially they want something to happen, and their street activity can best be understood as an attempt to maximize the chances of something interesting happening. Although the street activity is seen as boring, there is always the chance that something will happen the following night or week. The delinquency undertaken by these youths is the result of certain actions which they feel are not very remarkable, based around the search for a bit of interest and excitement.

Football hooliganism

Professional football matches offer contemporary youth, particularly working-class youth, an opportunity to identify with one another as a solid group in opposition to other such groups. It offers an opportunity to engage in group delinquency and, occasionally, in group fights. And as we saw in our review of the history of delinquency, this has been the case throughout this century. Football hooliganism is not a particularly new phenomenon, nor is it a peculiarly British problem, it has occurred all over the world.

Research into football hooliganism by **Williams, Dunning and Murphy** from Leicester University suggests that many of the common explanations for hooliganism, such as alcohol, violence on the pitch, the lack of all-seater stadiums, are too simplistic. The fact that the problem has persisted throughout this century indicates that its roots are deeper. Hooligan fans are predominantly from lower working-class backgrounds. One of the characteristic features of their communities is the street-based group activity. Such communities emphasise the ties of territory and the ability to 'defend' it. Also, due in part to increasing media attention, delinquent-prone youths who are more interested in fighting than football see the terrace 'ends' as places to maintain and improve tough reputations. Just as rival groups from different parts of a town or different estates will defend their areas, so they will join together to defend their 'end' of the football ground from fans from other towns. In fact, the chants and taunts of supporters are as much about the merits and demerits of the areas or towns as about the particular teams. Arsenal, for example, sing 'Maybe it's Because I'm a Londoner' and Leeds United chant 'York-shire', with both sets of supporters mimicking the other's accents.

At international level, such local support is subordinated to the national reputation and hooligan fans from different clubs will join forces. Certainly, the fans of the English national team have earned an unenviable reputation around the football-playing world. While football hooliganism is not solely an 'English disease', to be an English supporter at a match abroad clearly has a powerful image that attracts many young fans, an image which sees local fans and passers-by retreating in terror, and which has, it must be said, little to do with the achievements of the English football team itself. As Williams and colleagues indicate, the struggle for national pride can be exciting and intoxicating, especially in comparison to the everyday life of most of the hooligan fans.

To return to football hooliganism in Britain itself, it is clear that the existence of 'ends' at football grounds all over the country plays a central part in maintaining working-class boys' street-based culture. What goes on at these 'ends' is intelligible only to those involved. People from a wide range of social backgrounds go to watch football, but their interest and involvement will not be the same as the hooligan fans. As Corrigan puts it, the young supporter 'knows that a crowd of teachers chanting "We hate Nottingham Forest" is just not on'.

Violence at football matches has been explained in terms of the changing nature of the game itself and of the relationship between football clubs, and their players, and the communities in which they exist. The close identity between fans and their club has weakened as football has become big business and as the players, who were once from the same working-class community as the fans, have become rich superstars. Thus, it has been suggested that the attempts to re-organise football in a more businesslike manner, to make it more professional, have alienated young working-class fans from their football clubs. Hooliganism on the terraces can be seen as an organised resistance to such changes. Chanting, taking territory and violence have extended the contest of the game onto the terraces.

From this viewpoint, football violence has been given a new meaning since the early 1960s. It is a sign of the young fans commitment to their side's cause, and also an attempt to resist changes in the organisation of football. The changing relation of football, and the football club, to working-class culture is seen as an aspect of the wider decomposition of the traditional working-class community. However, this sort of explanation does not seem to hold up in the face of evidence that football hooliganism is by no means a uniquely modern, post-1960 occurrence.

The history of Glasgow Rangers Football Club, for example, makes it clear that riots, violence and vandalism have been well-established since at least the 1870s. This suggests that theories linking football hooliganism to changes in working-class community life are based on a somewhat dubious history. Working-class community life is as strongly established in Glasgow as anywhere, and football violence has occurred there for over a century. Similarly, in England football hooliganism has a long history. In the twenty years prior to the First World War there were numerous incidents of football hooliganism. The Football Association recorded 116 occasions between 1894 and

1914 when English league clubs were disciplined for trouble at their grounds. These occasions would clearly refer only to the more serious incidents where the Football Association felt it necessary to discipline clubs formally, and many more examples of hooliganism can be found in the newspapers of the period. Such evidence indicates that a whole range of disorderly behaviour occurred at football grounds during this period – missile throwing, pitch invasions and other supposedly 'contemporary' phenomena.

Let us look more closely at the football hooligans themselves. A study of the fans of Oxford United and Millwall found that actual physical violence played only a small part in life on the terraces (**Marsh, Rosser and Harre,** 1978). This study centred on the group nature and aspects of football support and of delinquency at football matches. As we have seen, the sense of territory is a crucial aspect of this behaviour. Each football ground has a distinct area or 'end' for the (generally young) home supporters, and these ends acquire distinctive names – the North Bank of Arsenal, The Stretford End of Manchester United, for example. The distinctive nature of the ends is reinforced by the fact that the occupants are often physically confined to the particular area for the whole of the football match. In more and more grounds, fences and grilles have been built around the 'ends' and the areas set aside for the visiting supporters, further highlighting the sense of territory.

Marsh and colleagues found that there was a clear and established career structure among the youths on the terraces. To begin with, there were the 'Novices', young boys of around 9, 10 and 11, who stood at the front of the 'end' and whose major occupation consisted of watching the activities of the older youths behind them. Then there were the 'Rowdies', boys of 15 and 16, who were the most identifiable group by virtue of their appearance, the noise they made and their tendency to run around the most. Lastly, were the 'Town Boys', older boys and young men up to the age of 25 or so, who had previously demonstrated their 'worth' in the Rowdies; who rested on their reputations but would still participate in acts of violence if called upon. Eventually, this group would move to other parts of the ground to watch the match with wives and girl-friends. In this division or career framework it is the Rowdies who are the typical football hooligans. Within this group there are a series of distinct and specialised roles, such as 'chant leader', 'aggro leader' or 'nutter'. The fact that such roles are well established would seem to demonstrate that football fans such as 'Rowdies' cannot be viewed simply as a bunch of disordered maniacs. The group is ordered and structured, as are its activities. For example, the members of the Rowdies group were well aware of their positions, and where they stood in relation to one another was clearly defined.

This career framework should not be seen as being wholly rigid or fixed. It is only used as a pattern for understanding the organisation of terrace life for young supporters. Many fans drift into and out of groups rather than making a gradual progress. Furthermore, the fans themselves, although recognising the different types of football supporter, will not think in terms of a career structure. Nevertheless, the notion of career structures can help to explain behaviour which might otherwise appear irrational and disorganised; it places the activity of the individual within the wider context of age and class dimensions. The activities of delinquent fans might be more intelligible if they can be related to particular roles and positions with respect to other fans.

To summarise, the seemingly disordered nature of football hooliganism can be seen as conforming to a distinct and orderly system of roles, rules and shared meanings. What the football terraces offer young working-class males is a chance to escape the boring world of their everyday life. They see the terraces as potentially dangerous and exciting. However, these fans know that the terraces are not really dangerous, thus this sense of adventure and danger has to be constructed and exaggerated. This exaggerations is well illustrated in a visit by Oxford United fans to the ground of their arch-rivals Swindon Town. The fans knew that very little had happened at the match, but on the way back in the coach, they constructed a much more exciting picture, aided by songs, 'We took Swindon and all of them in it, We took Swindon in half a minute. . . ' By the time the coach arrived back at Oxford the day had been made remarkable and worthy of being talked about.

Of course, the fact that structure and rules are to be found within the behaviour of football hooligans does not mean that there are no problems at football terraces and that such behaviour is to be condoned. We are not trying to excuse the behaviour, but to explain it. Social order can be found in events that are generally seen as dangerous and irrational.

Crime as a working-class phenomenon

This section will question the presumption that crime is over-whelmingly perpetrated by the working classes, or that the 'real' and serious crimes are those which are typically committed by this group – crimes like burglary, robbery and vandalism.

The official criminal statistics present a picture of crime as being predominantly a working-class phenomenon. However, these statistics probably underestimate the extend of middle and upper-class criminality to a much greater extent than they underestimate crime in general. While prosecuted crime may be largely working class, whether crime as a wider category is so is rather debateable, given that a large amount of middle and upper-class criminality goes undetected. Moreover, even when it is detected, it is often not formally and legally dealt with (the middle class bias in criminal statistics will be discussed in more detail in Chapter Four).

Crimes which are committed by those in higher positions in the social stratification system are commonly referred to as *white-collar crimes*. Originally the term referred to 'business' crime, but is now generally attributed to any crimes of the middle classes. **Edwin Sutherland's** famous pioneering work in 1940 produced evidence that white-collar crime might be sub-stantially underestimated in official criminal statistics. He found that petty crimes of stealing from work, and the more major crimes of bribery and corruption, often passed unnoticed or were dealt with informally and unofficially by firms. White-collar crime appeared to be a normal and accepted part of business practice, being both very costly and highly organised. Virtually all the largest American corporations broke the law in one way or another; laws controlling pollution, the adulteration of products, the regulating of prices and so on were ignored and broken at will.

The work of Sutherland, and later writers, clearly makes it difficult to identify crime with lower social status, with poverty, social problems and the like. Criminality is also linked with power, respectability and wealth. Below we will concentrate on an examination of corporate, business crime, the law-breaking of businesses and corporations. Such crimes will be used to illustrate the massive and largely unrealised extent of the 'crimes of the powerful'. We will also look briefly at the more trivial, but widespread, crimes of employee theft – 'fiddling at work' – as an example of another aspect of work-related crime.

Crimes of the powerful: corporate crime

The fact that criminality is linked with respectability and power is central to Marxist-based studies, such as those of Chambliss (see Chapter 2). In his book *On The Take*, **Chambliss** examines the social character of crime networks in Seattle, USA (Chambliss, 1978). His conclusion is that the forces behind organised crime in America are leading members of the ruling group, and the book's subtitle is 'From Petty Crooks to Presidents'. Chambliss's evidence is based on several years' participant observation in Seattle. After 'hanging around' bars in which gambling, drug and vice connections might be made and being involved with card schools, Chambliss found various contacts with inside knowledge. It was from these informants that he pieced together a picture of organised crime as being controlled by key personnel in the police force, local government, business and the legal profession. He goes on to argue that the emergence of organised crime networks is bound to happen in a capitalist system. Such a system stresses economic self-interest as all-important, rather than community spirit, public duty and so on; everybody is out for what they can get.

Looking at corporate crime generally, it is noticeable how such crime is greatly under-reported in the media, in comparison with 'conventional' crime. The most popular television crime series, such as *The Sweeney, Minder, The Professionals, Juliet Bravo, Hill Street Blues*, tend not to deal with corporate crime and the business criminal. As well as being neglected in popular entertainment, this type of crime has also been neglected as an area of study. It is not difficult to see why corporate crime has not received the same publicity as murder, robbery, theft, rape and so on – both in the mass media and in the study of crime. Corporate crime is not visible in the way that 'conventional' crime is, due to the complex nature of such crime and the ineffective laws and minimal punishments associated with it. Moreover, those who suffer from the effects of corporate crime, the victims, tend to remain unaware that they have been victimised. Their misfortune is often put down to being 'no one's fault' or an accident.

In his recent study of the links between power and crime, **Box** states that corporate crime is crime committed for the corporate organisation and not against it (Box, 1983). Thus, employee theft, including crimes of fraud against one's employer and embezzlement, are not included in his discussion of corporate crime. Corporate crime, then, refers to illegal acts (including acts of omission) of an individual or group within a legitimate formal organisation which are in accordance with the goals of that organisation. They must have some detrimental effect, either physical or economic, on employees, consumers or the general public. That definition, which is taken from Box's study, is rather long-winded, but corporate crime is a complex issue. The easiest way to understand the nature and extent of this type of crime is to look at some examples of the effect of specific corporate crimes.

Firstly, we should make the point that crime does not have to be intentional. Very serious consequences can and do follow from people or organisations being indifferent to the results of their actions. Indifference rather than intention may be the cause of greater human suffering, particularly with regard to corporate crime. It could be argued, in fact, that being indifferent to the consequences of one's actions indicates a high degree of contempt for (other) people.

It is important to realise that the law-breaking of large businesses and corporations can have severe consequences. It does not just refer to 'sharp business practices' and people making slightly greater profits than they should. There are numerous cases of corporate crime causing injury and death. To cite one example given by Box:

> Early in 1979, fifty people lost their lives as a result of an explosion aboard the tanker *Betelgeuse* whilst it was anchored at Bantry Bay in County Cork. An Inquiry headed by an Irish High Court Judge, Mr Justice Declan Costello, firmly placed the responsibility for this on two corporations, Total and Gulf, who deliberately decided not to carry out necessary repair

work costing a mere £130,000 because they intended to sell the tanker.

It is very difficult to assess accurately the costs of corporate crime. The economic costs are almost incomprehensibly large. It is not easy to grasp the financial significance of organisations diluting their products, for instance, so that many millions of customers are paying a few pence extra for their goods. While the few pence – or less – extra for the individual customer might seem insignificant, an organisation may be making a massive illegal profit. All studies of the economic costs of corporate crime agree that individuals are deprived of far more money by such crime than by the more conventional crimes of robbery and theft. There are also social costs which are, again, immeasurable. As well as corporate crime undermining the public's faith in the business world, it is also likely that crimes of bribery and corruption by large corporations affect the poorer, less powerful sections of society more than other sections. Powerful business institutions operate in a way that ensures their interests are given priority, rather than the interests of the less powerful sectors of the community. In general terms, then, corporate crime involves robbing the poor to benefit the rich. It rewards those who put self-interest ahead of the public interest.

Of course, corporate crime is actually carried out by individuals; organisations cannot themselves plan and commit crimes. Businessmen who commit corporate crime are not forced to do so. They will be able to weigh up the advantages of breaking a law and not doing so; and they will tend to choose the former path if it seems likely to secure economic and career advancement. One corporate lawyer said that he went along with producing false insurance policies without thinking anything of it, 'It was something the company needed done, that's all'. There are instances where individuals are caught between their conscience and the corporate policy, and occasionally between their conscience and their jobs. In explaining why he had gone along with 'doctoring' data so as to secure a contract deadline, a supervisor pointed out, 'If I refused to take part in the fraud, I would have to either resign or be fired'.

With regard to the control of corporate crime, there is little to deter the corporate criminal. Many such crimes are looked into by special regulatory bodies rather than the police. In the UK, there are factory inspectorates, railway inspectorates, monopolies and mergers commissions. Although such bodies have the power to recommend criminal prosecution, they are mainly concerned with the inspection and regulation of organisations. There is a fraud squad within the police force, but the majority of their work is concerned with employee theft rather than crimes committed by and for business organisations. Furthermore, the typical penalties for those individuals and organisations who are found guilty of corporate crime do little to deter the would-be criminal.

In addition, the skilful corporate law-breaker or law-bender will often be able to discover new schemes to avoid or get round criminal laws that are introduced to regulate particular corporate activities. Laws introduced to regulate corporate behaviour differ from most criminal laws in that they do not centre on the results of the breaking of the particular regulation. To give an example, a company was found responsible for a hoist accident at a power station in Kent in 1978 in which four people died and five were seriously injured. However, the company was not prosecuted for the fact that four people died, but because the machinery was not properly maintained; they were fined £5,000.

In conventional crime one is charged with the results of one's actions. As Box puts it, a person accused of stabbing someone is not likely just to be charged with 'carrying an offensive weapon'. This is not to say that businessmen should be responsible for all the indirect effects of their policies and actions, or that, for example, the individuals in the company responsible for the hoist accident described above should be charged and sentenced for murder. The point is that as the laws do not focus on the results of corporate crime, the corporate criminal need only worry about relatively lenient punishment for breaking a particular regulation, and not be concerned with the wider consequences of that action.

In concluding his discussion of corporate crime, Box raises the question of whether it can be justified to send thousands of people to prison each year because they are too poor to pay fines (in 1981, 20,000 males were imprisoned for defaulting on fine payments) when their crime is trivial in the extreme in comparison with corporate crime. While the powerful seem to get away with serious crimes, the powerless commit less serious offences and get prison.

Concluding our discussion of corporate crime, the existence of criminal corporations should also be mentioned. As well as crime *for* corporations and crimes *against* corporations (employee theft), there are corporations deliberately set up for the sole purpose of committing criminal activity. A study of long-firm fraud, one form of corporate crime, by Levi illustrates this type of criminal activity (Levi, 1981).

Long-firm fraud: an example of corporate crime

Over the past fifty years there has been a massive expansion in the extent and importance of fraud. Frauds comprise almost 5% of all recorded indictable (serious) crime in England and Wales, compared to only 0.5% in 1928. This expansion has imposed a strain on the control of fraud. In the metropolitan police there is only one fraud squad officer for every hundred officers. Moreover, fraud trials generally take longer than other criminal trials, due to the sophisticated and complex nature of many frauds, and they often stretch over many months.

Levi defines long-firm fraud as referring to businesses which order substantial quantities of goods on credit at a time when the owners of the business either intend not to pay for them or suspect that they will not be able to pay for them. The first record of the term 'long-firm fraud' which Levi uncovers was in a journal of 1869, while the obtaining of goods under the false pretence that one had an honest and solvent business is an activity with a much longer history. Long-firm frauds are to be found in most western countries, and are liable to occur wherever there is extensive use of credit in business transactions. Levi classifies various sub-types of such fraud, although for our purposes we will look at this type of corporate crime in general terms.

The background of long-firm fraudsters is far more varied than is found with convicted criminals as a whole. They include businessmen who have never before committed any substantial crime; people who make their living principally from fraud; and other professional criminals who engage in a range of crimes of which long-firm fraud is one.

The precise details and mechanics of long-firm fraud vary from case to case, and many are exceedingly complex. The basic pattern nevertheless remains the same. Looking at an example of one such fraud will indicate this basic procedure. The success of the fraudster often hinges on the ability to tell a convincing story. In the 1960s a man with an American accent arrived at a coastal resort in South Wales and announced that he represented an American corporation which wished to purchase a leisure and amusement arcade in the town. He offered a generous price which the owners of the arcade accepted. However, he explained that the money was temporarily tied up. While waiting for this money to come through, he asked the owners if they would allow him to order goods for the coming summer season. They agreed to this and even gave him their headed notepaper to use in ordering. He wrote to various suppliers implying that he owned the arcade and obtained around £350,000 worth of goods on credit. One night all these goods were secretly taken away and disappeared for good. The man's identity has never been discovered. In order to become a successful fraudster, these skills of being able to present a convincing front and remain calm under pressure have to become almost second nature.

As we suggested above, long-firm frauds can be carried out by people who have no social or business contact with the criminal fraternity. Like most upper-class criminals, the 'businessman-fraudster' can make large amounts of money from crime without every becoming a known or convicted criminal. The initial motivations that lead a previously 'honest' businessman to commit a long-firm fraud are liable to be financial, perhaps a temporary shortage of money. However, the more or less honest businessman who decides to commit a fraud 'just this once' may become excited by the fun and challenge of it, as well as by the material profits. The reasons given by those who take part in commercial crime rather than straight business tend to stress the pleasure involved in 'trying to beat the system', and the battle of wits with creditors, as well as the pleasure that the proceeds of crime bring.

Fraud is one of the risks which result from the spread of credit. However, fraud is only a minor commercial risk for most suppliers of goods and credit. It does not deter firms from supplying on credit, and there is always insurance cover to fall back on. Thus, although there has been an extension of fraud as credit facilities have expanded, this has not affected the central principle on which the regulation of fraud is based – that at all costs 'free enterprise' should not be discouraged by fear of prosecution. The result of this is that the law relating to fraud and commercial affairs in general is strictly limited in its scope.

Long-firm fraudsters seem to get treated more leniently by the police and the legal system than do 'conventional' criminals. Moreover, the complex nature of many frauds makes it difficult for the police to prepare a sound case. As one officer said to Levi: 'If we nicked everybody we thought might have done a long-firm, we'd never finish our paperwork, the cases might never come to court, and if they did, they'd never have the room to try them.'

As far as sentencing is concerned it would seem to be the case that long-firm fraudsters are sentenced on the basis that they are business law-breakers rather than 'villains'. Judges might find it easier to sympathise with and understand such law-breakers in comparison to other types of criminal. Furthermore, there is no shocked outcry from the mass media if such criminals are given relatively minor sentences. The amount of time that even 'professional' long-firm fraudsters spend in prison is remarkably small in relation to the generally large amounts of money that are obtained from such frauds (Reading 5, Chapter 5, taken from Levi's study, looks at the long-firm fraudster and imprisonment).

'Fiddling at work': employee theft

In this section we have concentrated on one type of white-collar crime, corporate crime. Before concluding, it would be useful to refer to the more common crime of employee theft, 'fiddling at work'. Clearly, the nature of theft will vary with different types of employment. To gain an impression of the extent of employee theft, we will look at a study of fiddling and pilferage at a medium-sized factory-production bakery in south-east England, undertaken by **Jason Ditton** (1977).

The idea that everyone 'makes a bit on the side' and 'has their little perks' was prevalent throughout the factory. As the night manager said, 'You've got to allow for losses. . .you get the odd loaf taken home and not paid for'. But always there is the implication that, 'we all make a bit on the side. . .know what I mean?'. Ditton worked in the bakery over vacations for a few years and reckoned that each man had an illegal income of about 10 per cent of his bread sales, very little of which appeared as a loss in the firm's financial records.

Rather than assuming that a few corrupt workers steal large amounts, it would seem more reasonable to contend that many, if not the majority, of employees regularly take small amounts. An American firm which used lie detectors on 1400 employees found that 62 per cent admitted petty theft before the tests were administered and a further 14 per cent after. This finding has been supported by various other firms and factories.

To return to Ditton's study, skill at fiddling customers was a major criteria of unofficial status among the bread salesmen. This fiddling included overcharging, increasing the price of bread to unknowing customers, and keeping the price the same but reducing the size of the bread delivery. Also, the salesmen distinguished between those on their rounds who should not be fiddled (such as disabled people, ex-salesmen) and those who qualified as 'fair game'. This distinction can be seen as allowing the salesmen to defend themselves through providing a justifica- tion for fiddling. Of course, this is common to many criminals who define the victim of their criminality as being rich enough to withstand the loss. It is almost a Robin Hood notion: 'you don't feel so guilty with big stores. . .they allow wastage'.

Generally, most of the men did feel some guilt and disliked fiddling, but said, 'I don't like it but I have to'. On the other hand, this guilt is reduced by counter accusations of 'they deserve it' and the like. Furthermore, maxims such as 'look after number one' and 'it's a dog eat dog world' are taken by fiddlers as principles for action. If it is discovered, employee theft is one of the least stigmatised of crimes. In Ditton's study, the majority of offenders were dealt with quickly and leniently – 'Put that bloody loaf down' or 'Don't you try and fiddle me' being examples of reactions. The workers who were fiddling at this particular factory were able to keep their self-image and conduct their working lives as good citizens; like most unconvicted white-collar criminals they were not stigmatised. Two extracts from Mars' recent study of workplace crime which illustrate the wide range of fiddling at work are included as readings in Chapter 5 (Readings 6 and 7).

Crime as a male phenomenon

Here we will examine the supposition – supported by statistics on sex differences in crime – that crime is characteristically a male activity. We will look at sociological explanations for the under-representation of females in criminal activity. Table 3.1 below shows the ratio of females to males convicted for certain crimes and makes clear the male domination of criminality. Only in the crime of shoplifting does the ratio of females convicted even approach that of males.

Table 3.1   The ratio of conviction between females and males for selected crimes, England and Wales, 1979

Indictable crime	Female/Male ratio for population aged 14–65 years
Shoplifting	.802
Fraud and forgery	.221
Handling stolen goods	.157
Murder/manslaughter, attempted etc.	.125
Thefts (excluding shoplifting)	.112
Woundings and serious assaults	.086
Criminal damage	.070
Robbery	.057
Burglary	.039
Sex offences	.011
All indictable crimes	.178

(NB a ratio of 1.00 would indicate an equal proportion of male and female offenders)

While the vast majority of offenders are men, a small proportion are women. It is sometimes claimed that female criminal activity is restricted to limited types of crimes. However, women do in fact contribute to all kinds of offences. The most common offences for both sexes are crimes against property, with shoplifting being regarded as the 'typical' female offence (although adolescent males also indulge in this particular form of crime in significantly high numbers). Women tend to commit few crimes of violence, and those which do occur are mainly committed within the confines of the family.

We will break down and discuss two basic, possible explanations for these marked differences between the crime figures for men and women: firstly, that women do not indulge in criminality to the same extent as men; secondly, that female crime is greatly underestimated by the statistics, in other words there is more female crime than the statistics indicate.

Women do not indulge in criminality to the same extent as men

Biological and psychological arguments

These arguments suggest that the biological and/or psychological make-up of women does not predispose them to criminality to the same extent as men. Until recently differences in the rate of crime between the sexes was generally explained as being due to biological or psychological differences.

Lombroso, whose somewhat bizarre theories of crime and criminals we looked at in Chapter Two, claimed that 'a delinquent woman is more unnatural than a delinquent man'. He argued that criminals were physically distinguishable by, for example, large jaws, high cheek bones, extra toes and so on. He found fewer of these traits in women, which led him to assert that women are 'congenitally less inclined to crime than men'. Furthermore, women who did commit crime were seen as not feminine. He suggested that women are by nature passive and therefore less inclined to crime than men – although such a suggestion does not take acount of the fact that by no means all crimes involve violence.

Lombroso's work is dated (*The Female Offender* by Lombroso and Ferrero was originally published in 1895) and largely discredited. However, the biological argument that women are naturally averse to crime and that female criminals are in some way maladjusted has never been fully adandoned. A series of studies, usually by men, have argued that the female biology determines their temperament or personality, and makes women more passive and timid. Female criminals are often seen as suffering from some physical or mental pathology (disease) and the courts still accept the arguments, that female offenders have biological problems, with the menopause, pregnancy, pre-menstrual tension and so on regularly used as explanations or excuses for their criminality. There is little evidence to support such explanations, which are insulting to women in that they are viewed as faulty biological mechanisms which spend some of their time malfunctioning.

There are a number of problems to be found in the attempts to explain the low level of female crime as being due to physical or mental maladjustment. The female personality is not biologically determined, as researches in different cultures have shown. The female (and male) personality and behaviour is culturally determined, through the socialisation process. Moreover, these interpretations emphasise too heavily individual rather than social causes of crime and delinquency. They tend to restrict the causes of criminality to hereditary characteristics and overlook the effects of environmenal influences and cultural traditions. Finally, as we have shown earlier, what is defined as criminal varies across time and place, thus making it difficult to argue that in-built differences between the sexes can explain what is a variable phenomena.

Patterns of socialisation and social control

The basic argument with which we are concerned here is that the low level of female crime is a result of the expectations and constraints that are placed on women by society. Traditionally, women have been viewed as dependent and passive, and males as aggressive and assertive. The socialisation process tends to emphasise these conventional views. This is especially the case among the working class in that working-class females most strongly represent and support traditional sex roles. A study of working-class girls by Sue Sharpe demonstrated that their main aims and priorities were to marry, have children and settle down (Sharpe, 1976). Moves toward emancipation and liberation started, and have largely remained, with middle-class women.

Different role expectations for men and women lead to different patterns and practices of socialisation. Men, rather than women, learn the skills necessary for certain types of criminal activity. Boys learn how to fight and handle guns, and have the strength required to break into houses. Burglary, for example, is an untypical female crime, as it requires the criminal to be out alone on the streets at night, and to possess 'masculine' skills such as the ability to force an entry.

Linked with socialisation is social control. There is often stronger social control evident in the socialisation of girls in comparison to boys. Girls are expected to conform to a stricter morality, by their parents in particular. They are likely to be allowed less freedom to go out on the streets and stay out late. It is argued that this is a significant factor in reducing the likelihood of girls joining delinquent groups. Thus, adolescent boys are out on the streets and more likely to join gangs, and this is where they can become involved in minor law-breaking which may lead to more serious criminality. If it is more heavily impressed on girls that certain types of behaviour are wrong, then they will tend to feel greater apprehension and guilt if they are tempted by delinquent or criminal activities. The basic argument is that the more adolescents are supervised by their parents and, perhaps, their teachers, the less likely they are to become involved with or influenced by delinquent contemporaries and delinquent values. Girls are generally more closely controlled and supervised by their parents. Hoffman-Bustamente has argued that these differing patterns of socialisation and social control for boys and girls have tended to concentrate those women who do break the law into certain categories of offence. In particular, criminal behaviour in women tends to involve non-violent crimes which do not involve the use of physical strength or agility, since women have not been 'trained' to develop such skills (Hoffman–Bustamente D.Y., 'The nature of female criminality', *Issues in Criminology* 8, 2, 1973).

It may be that with greater equality and emancipation the proportion of female criminals will rise. As women take greater advantage of educational and occupational opportunities so sex differences in the level of criminal activity may diminish. If this does occur there is a danger that womens' movements will be blamed for the rise in the female crime rate, and that this may be used to argue against further female emancipation. Certainly, there is evidence that the number of women convicted of assaults, woundings and violent crime has risen over the last two decades. Generally, there has been a rise in the female crime rate, especially in the 14–21 age group. However, such statistics can be misleading. It could be that teenage girls nowadays act in a more self-confident manner, and that this fuels notions that they are becoming more violent. This then becomes a *self-fulfilling prophecy*, police officers, magistrates and social workers will be more likely to be stricter with female offenders; and thus more females will be convicted of crimes.

Although there is no evidence that liberation has led to greater female criminality, such a view is widely held and has been strongly expressed in the popular press. The *Sun* reported a 'Crime Wave of the "Lib" Girls' (1 September, 1975), while the *Daily Mail* claimed that 'Women's Lib "pushes up crime"' (1 February, 1980). But it is not just the popular press who have argued such a case. For example The *Sunday Times* has asserted that, 'In recent years we've experienced a new, aggressive, liberated criminality in women' (30 March, 1980).

There is not doubt that the behaviour of the police and the courts, as well as the wider public, will be influenced by their image of female crime. If this image has changed because of the way the media has portrayed female crime, and linked liberation with violent crime, then women are liable to be treated more severely by the police and the courts. This will, of course, push up the female crime figures.

Opportunities for crime

Differing roles without society limit or increase opportunities to commit crime. It is still the case that the majority of girls do not see themselves as primarily workers or careerists. As was suggested above, girls have been socialised into viewing work as secondary to marriage and child-rearing. If women's careers and position in society generally confine them to the home, they will have less opportunity to commit crimes which are associated with work, such as fraud. Employee theft, after all, is impossible if one is not employed. Because women are largely confined to jobs with low status and power, they will be relatively less able to engage in serious forms of white-collar and corporate crime. In addition, the fact that women are less mobile than men and more confined to the home means that they are less likely to be exposed to situations which lack effective informal social controls.

In areas where women have similar opportunities to men they appear as likely to break laws. The high incidence of shoplifting among women, for example, reflects the day-to-day activities in which female criminality is liable to be expressed. In the world of organised, professional crime, sex-segregation is the norm. Women are likely to be viewed in terms of traditional sex-role stereotypes, as unreliable, emotional, illogical and so on. Moreover, male criminals tend to see the crimes they commit as too dangerous for women, or too difficult, or their masculine pride may not be willing to accept women as organisers of crime, as 'bosses'.

Female crime is greatly underestimated by the criminal statistics

The issue here is whether the statistics on female crime provide an accurate picture of the actual extent of such crime. There are a number of points and arguments worth considering. The more minor crimes are less liable to be known to the police and recorded in the statistics than are serious crimes. Thus, if women tend to commit more minor crimes, they will have a much better chance of avoiding detection.

With regard to crimes that are known about, the police and courts may be more lenient with female offenders. For example, when deciding whether to caution, arrest or charge an individual, the police may be influenced by the sex of the offender. The stereotypical views held by agents of social control will tend to suggest that women are less delinquent and crime-prone than men, that they are not 'real' criminals. Females are less likely than males to be labelled as delinquent and to be processed accordingly. Also, the fact that police officers will know that female crime rates are lower than male crime rates will further incline them to the view that women are not by nature 'criminal types'. If women are convicted of crimes in greater numbers (and, as mentioned, female convictions have increased in recent years), it will be interesting to see how the police and the courts react.

The male prison population vastly outnumbers the female; in 1979, 143,000 males spent some time in prison, in comparison to 8,000 females. Thus, if convicted, women are far less likely to be given a custodial sentence. One reason for this is that more women are first offenders, who are generally treated more leniently. However, the reluctance of sentencers to imprison women does not seem to be based on any clear principles, given the supposed principle of equality before the law. An example of this differential sentencing policy was reported in the *Guardian* 18 August, 1980, which quoted a male judge, who told a female defendent, 'If you were a man I would send you to prison without hesitation'. The more lenient punishments given to women probably reflect a belief that female crime is a result of sickness, of some physical or emotional problem, rather than being rational action with specific, often financial, motives. In other words, the old view that women's crime is physically explainable would still appear to be influential, despite the fact that there is no real evidence for such explanations.

Another point to consider in relation to the statistics on female crime is the view that men may adopt a more chivalrous attitude to women, based on misconceptions of women as passive and gentle. Therefore, the police, magistrates and judges, who are all predominantly male, will tend to leniency. If a woman is tearful and apologetic and can claim some biological disturbance, then she is not likely to be treated as severely as a man.

So far we have looked at the view that sex differences affect the way in which the police and the courts act toward offenders, and that this enables women to escape criminalisation to a greater extent than men. However, it has also been argued that women are discriminated against by the agents of the law, just as they are in other areas of life. It is maintained that the courts, in particular, view young females as in need of 'protection'. Thus, young female offenders are more likely to be placed in protective and custodial institutions than are boys whose delinquent or criminal behaviour is similar. Boys are left in the community because they are not felt to need such protection. These arguments, however, refer to the less serious, juvenile criminality. They do not necessarily contradict the view that for more serious crimes women are less severely treated then men. As we have mentioned, judges, the police and the public may have more difficulty in understanding serious female crime and tend to believe that the woman offender is not really criminal. Her action is seen as an irrational or emotional response to a particular situation; she 'only did it for love', for example.

Overall, however, the bulk of evidence on female crime suggests that sex plays a relatively minor role in determining the response of the legal system. There is no clear evidence that women receive massively more favourable treatment from the police or the courts. Thus, we would suggest that these second types of explanation for the differences in the rate of crime between men and women – that female crime exists to a much greater extent than is indicated by the statistics but is just less often recorded – cannot explain the enormous sex differences in recorded rates of crime.

It would appear that the explanation for the strong link between sex and crime must lie in the wider stratification system in society. Women are far more restricted than men in their access to the reward structure of society, and women are still largely restricted to the private, family sphere. In contrast, crime, when it is recorded, is a public occurrence. The continuing importance of sexual divisions in employment and of traditional stereotypes of the woman's role are central to explanations for sexual divisions in the sphere of criminality.

In this chapter we have looked at specific aspects and illustrations of crime and the study of it. In the next chapter we will examine in greater detail the statistics on crime. In doing so we shall return to some of the issues raised above, including the question of class and sex biases in these statistics.

PART 3

Statistical data and documentary readings

4 Measuring crime: criminal statistics

In popular debate about crime one issue always comes to the fore: how much crime is there in our society, and is it increasing or decreasing? To answer these questions people invariably turn to the official criminal statistics which are collected and published by the Home Office. In this chapter we will examine what these statistics show and discuss the extent to which they provide an accurate picture of the range and extent of criminal behaviour.

Criminal statistics are usually quoted as 'hard facts'; that is, they are accepted unquestioningly, and are often used to support the view that there is a rapidly increasing rate of serious crime in modern society. It is also important to recognise that it is on the basis of these statistics that important decisions are made by governments in relation to their policies towards crime and its treatment. Decisions concerning the most effective and efficient way of allocating resources (of money and manpower) in the attempt to deal with crime–related social problems will be influenced by criminal statistics. For example, in 1980 the Home Secretary, William Whitelaw, introduced the 'short, sharp, shock' punishments for young offenders, involving a few months' strict discipline and almost para-military training in detention centres. This widely publicised policy was intended to relieve public concern over the rise in violent crimes against persons and property committed by juveniles.

However, the questions we should keep in mind during our examination of criminal statistics are whether they really justify such public concern, and, most importantly, what do they *really* tell us? The first section of the chapter will provide an overview of patterns and trends in criminal behaviour, as indicated by the official criminal statistics. In the second section problems associated with the use of these statisics will be examined.

The pattern of crime

Broadly speaking, the official statistics indicate that there is an increasing rate of crime, and that the increase has accelerated rapidly in the post-war period, especially since the mid-1950s. Figure 4.1 summarises the total number of serious offences per 100,000 of the population for the period 1957 to 1977, and shows a 290 per cent increase over those two decades. In 1900 the police in England and Wales recorded less than *three* crimes for every *thousand* of the population. By 1974, however, they recorded *four* crimes for every *hundred* of the population – a thirteen-fold increase in seventy odd years (Radzinowicz, L. and King, J., *The Growth of Crime*, 1977).

Figure 4.1 *Indictable offences per 100,000 population, 1957–77.*

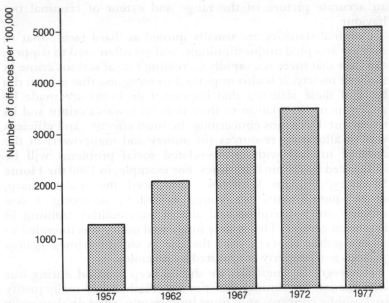

Source: *Criminal Statistics, England and Wales, 1979,* HMSO, 1980

While this increase is startling, it is worth noting that a concern over 'crime waves', and rising levels of juvenile crime in particular, is not a new phenomenon. In parts of London during the last century, for example, it was certainly not safe to walk the streets at night, with violence and robbery commonplace, as the stories of Charles Dickens illustrate.

So, while criminal statistics have risen substantially, theft and violence is clearly not a modern problem. So far as the type of crime committed is concerned throughout this century the great bulk of crime has always involved stealing of one kind or another. Simple theft is still the commonest variety of stealing. But there have been significant changes in the nature of stealing since the Second World War. In particular, there has been a major and disproportionate increase in shoplifting (3 per cent of theft in 1945, compared with 14 per cent in 1978) and in thefts from, and of, motor vehicles. Crimes of violence comprise less than 4 per cent of recorded crime, and while crimes of violence have risen rapidly in numbers in the post-war period there have been changes in the pattern of such offences. In 1945, 28 per cent of violent crimes against the person were of the most serious nature – such as serious wounding or homicide – but by 1975 this proportion had dropped to 9 per cent, and by 1979 to 6 per cent. The main factor causing this redistribution seems to have been a massive increase in non-serious wounding.

Thus, it is indisputable that the volume of *recorded* crime has risen. However, the statistics indicate that criminal activity is not randomly distributed throughout the whole population, and we need to examine the *social incidence* of recorded crime. According to the figures, the people most likely to commit criminal offences in Britain live in urban areas, are young, male and working class. We will look briefly at each of these elements in turn.

Urban/rural differences

The crime rate is higher in urban areas than it is in rural areas, and the larger the urban area the greater the crime rate is. Thus, London and other large cities have higher rates of crime per 100,000 of population than do smaller and medium-sized towns. However, although the rates of crime in the large cities have always exceeded the rates in rural areas, the increase in crime rates this century has been a universal phenomenon. In other

Table 4.1 Indictable offences known to the police per 1,000 population for selected years and police forces.

Police Force	1921	1931	1938	1953	1971
Metropolitan Police	2.3	3.2	11.0	11.9	43.1
Birmingham	1.6	3.4	6.2	11.7	48.6
Liverpool and Bootle	12.4	14.1	16.1	22.4	73.9
Manchester and Salford	2.8	4.2	6.2	21.0	84.0
Devon and Cornwall	1.7	3.5	5.6	10.2	26.0
Suffolk	1.4	1.7	2.9	8.8	21.2

Source: M. Rutter and H. Giller, *Juvenile Delinquency: trends and perspectives* (1983), using data provided by Home Office

words, there has been a large proportional increase in recorded crime in all parts of the country, as Table 4.1 illustrates. The figures shows an increase in crime rates for all areas, yet there are curious differences in the extent and timing of the change in such rates in different police forces. The crime rate in Liverpool/ Bootle in 1921 and 1931 was several times the rate in Manchester/ Salford, for example, but the massive increases in that area between 1938 and 1971 put it above the Liverpool area by 1971. Students might find it useful to examine and discuss the figures in Table 4.1; it should be born in mind, however, that definitions of indictable crimes have changed over time, as we mentioned in Chapter 1.

In spite of the variations, crime rates are significantly higher in urban areas than in rural areas. This might be the result of a number of factors, assuming, of course, that urban dwellers are not inherently more devious and criminal than rural dwellers:

THE ROLE OF OPPORTUNITY
Large urban areas afford greater opportunities for criminal activity with the presence of large department stores, ware-houses, financial institiutions, large car parks and so on.

THE CHARACTERISTICS OF THE COMMUNITY
It is likely to be easier to commit crime in urban areas in that it is easier to be unnoticed and to remain anonymous in such areas. In rural areas there is a tendency for many of the inhabitants to know one another; strangers are highly visible and liable to cause suspicion. In urban areas, therefore, the effectiveness of informal

social control is reduced. In rural areas it might be that people will tell the parents of youths whom they see committing some offence; and although crimes may be committed they will often be dealt with informally and so will not figure in the criminal statistics.

POLICE PROCEDURE

In rural areas the police tend to be more integrated with the community. They are more likely to know offenders personally, or to know their families, and thus to warn rather than 'book' offenders. This is, of course, only a tendency, and the move away from local policemen to larger, centralised policing may reduce this effect. Reading 9 in Chapter 5, from Cain's study of rural and urban police forces, illustrates very distinctly the differing styles of policing in different areas.

Age differences

In both sexes criminal activity appears to peak in adolescence and early adulthood – between the ages of 14, and younger, and 21. In 1977, 8 per cent of males aged 14 to under 17 were found guilty of, or cautioned for, offences; in comparison with 0.7 per cent of the 30+ age group. Similarly, in 1977, 1.6 per cent of females aged 14 to under 17 were found guilty of, or cautioned for, offences; in comparison with 0.2 per cent of females in the 30+ age group.

This does not mean that people become more honest as they grow older. It is more likely that the types of crime committed by older people will be less noticed and less liable to be recorded in the criminal statistics. Older people spend less time out of the house, on the street where the bulk of criminal activity occurs. To take a somewhat simplistic example, stealing low-priced goods from shops is more likely to be reported than stealing goods of equal value from one's place of work. Having said that, as the figures given above indicate, the younger age groups, the 14 to under 17's followed closely by the 17 to under 21's, contain far higher proportions of people who are found guilty of, or cautioned for, criminal offences than do older age groups. With regard to theft, for example, in 1970 38 per cent of persons convicted of theft were juveniles (that is, under 17).

However, a couple of points should be made about these statistics. Firstly, the peak age for conviction is around the school-leaving age and the likelihood of conviction after that age declines; and, secondly, a very significant proportion of the offences committed by juveniles are very trivial – stealing milk bottles for example.

It is popularly held that juvenile delinquency is on the increase. Certainly there have been fears in the media over a 'new school-age crime wave'. Recent statistics issued by the Metropolitan Police indicated that a quarter of all serious crimes in Greater London are committed by school-children. One arrest in four is of persons aged 10–16 years and half of all arrests are of persons under 21 years. As we have already pointed out, the crime rate in general is increasing for all age groups, and there is little evidence that juvenile criminality is increasing at a very much greater rate than crime in general. Between 1959 and 1977 the number of offences per 100,000 of the population for males aged 14 to under 17 increased by 148 per cent, compared to a rise of 136 per cent for males aged 21 and over – hardly a massive difference. What seems to have happened over the last twenty years or so is that a higher proportion of juveniles are being dealt with officially by the police rather than being dealt with unofficially or warned. Thus higher proportions of juveniles are figuring in the criminal statistics.

Sex differences

Criminal statistics in all countries have consistently shown that more males than females appear before the courts and are convicted for criminal activities. Of all offenders found guilty, in all courts, both magistrate and crown courts, females make up approximately 11 per cent of the total (magistrate courts deal with relatively minor crimes and civil actions, whereas the more serious indictable offences, which can be tried by jury, are dealt with by crown courts). Females make up an even smaller proportion of the prison population in this country, between 3 and 4 per cent at any one time. Furthermore, 12 per cent of males compared to 2 per cent of females are found guilty of, or cautioned for, criminal offences by the age of 17.

Statistics also show that while the crime rate has increased regularly for all groups, the rise in female crime has been far steeper than the rise in male crime. Between 1959 and 1977, the number of female offenders per 100,000 of the population aged 14 to under 17 increased by 379 per cent (compared to a 148 per cent increase for males of the same age group). For females aged over 21 there was a 281 per cent increase (compared to 136 per cent for males of the same age group).

Although male offenders still heavily outnumber female offenders, these changes have led to an alteration in the male–female ratio for crime and delinquency. Figure 4.2 shows the changed male–female ratio for the 14 to 17 age group. In 1957 the ratio was 10.79 to 1, but by 1977 it had fallen to 4.97 to 1.

In Chapter 3, we looked at explanations for the differences in male and female criminality. This section has just presented some statistical data on such differences.

Figure 4.2   Male–Female ratio for indictable offences in 14–17 year olds.

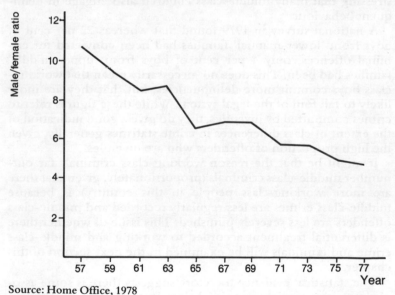

Source: Home Office, 1978

Class differences

The fourth element in the pattern of criminal statistics is that recorded crime is largely a working-class phenomenon.

Although crime occurs across all social classes, and is not just restricted to individuals from working-class backgrounds, official statistics show a clear link between social class and crime.

It has been a long and widely held assumption that crime is very much more frequent among those of low social status. Furthermore, this presumed strong association between crime and social class has been the basis for most of the leading sociological theories of crime. In our discussion of theories of crime, in Chapter Two, we examined various theoretical approaches which centred on class differences in crime and, in particular, juvenile delinquency. For example, the Functionalist-based theories see crime and delinquency as a reponse to frustrations arising from lower social position and status. Although a range of sociological theories has suggested that crime is due to deprivation of one sort or another, it is worth stressing that many middle-class children also engage in delinquent behaviour.

A national survey in 1979 found that whereas 22 per cent of boys from 'lower-manual' families had been convicted for criminal offences, only 4 per cent of boys from 'upper-middle' families had been. This does not necessarily mean that working-class boys commit more delinquencies, but that they are more likely to fall foul of the legal system. While these figures refer to crimes committed by juveniles, they do give a good indication of the extent of class differences in crime statistics generally, given the high proportion of offenders who are juveniles.

It might be that the reason working-class criminals far outnumber middle-class criminals (proportionately, given that there are more working-class people in this country) is because middle-class crimes are less regularly recorded and middle-class offenders are less severely punished. This issue of whether there is differential treatment accorded to working and middle-class crime and criminals will be examined in the next section of this chapter.

The statistical evidence therefore suggests there is some association between crime and social class. But whilst this association is most noticeable between the extremes of the social class scale, it is far less marked between the middle groups. The national survey referred to above, for instance, found that both the 'lower-middle' and 'upper-manual' groups had the same rates of delinquency – 12 per cent. One final point on the relationship of social class to crime: it may not be low social class in itself which is associated with crime, but rather that low social class is liable to be linked with other factors, perhaps parental criminality, deprivation or inadequacy of some kind, which might predispose individuals brought up in certain social classes toward criminality.

Having given a brief overview of the social incidence, or the pattern of recorded crime, we will turn now to some of the problems involved in the use of criminal statistics.

A critique of official criminal statistics

Official crime figures provide a classic example of why social scientists should treat statistics on social problems with suspicion. As a general point, statistics are social products, in that they are produced for organisations and governments. They are often organised and structured in the interests of influential and powerful bodies in order to make a particular point, perhaps to make a case for more money or resources, or to show a particular body or organisation in a good light.

Although the validity of official crime statistics has been questioned and doubted, they nevertheless provide an important basis for people's ideas about crime and criminals. But in fact there are two major and important deficiences with them. Firstly, there is the problem of *omission*: only a proportion of crimes and offenders are included in the official figures. Secondly, there is the problem of *bias* – in that those crimes and offenders included in the statistics might not be a representative picture of all crime and of all offenders. We will consider, firstly, the question of omission; then we will examine the issues concerned with bias in the statistics; and thirdly we will look at attempts to overcome some of the problems with the official criminal statistics.

The 'dark figure' of unrecorded crime

Criminal acts are defined by the Home Office as 'those acts against the law for which the offender is caught, tried and found guilty'. This obviously represents only a proportion of criminal activity in Britain since a number of crimes remain undetected and a number of offenders are not convicted.

In particular, criminal statistics only show what police forces record, and the police clearly cannot be expected to record the numerous offences which they do not know about. Criminal statistics, therefore, only indicate the crimes that are reported to the police and recorded by them as crimes. On top of this, there also exists what is termed a 'dark figure' of unrecorded crime. The bulk of this non-recording is due to crime not being reported to the police. However, it is also the case that not all events reported to the police as crimes are treated by them, and recorded, as crimes. A significant proportion of crime reports are subsequently written off as 'no crimes'. Furthermore, the role of the police is crucial in determining whether offences that they do know about are proceeded against. It is the police who have to decide whether the unruly pickets or drug users they pick up are prosecuted; and if the police took every offender to court the legal system would not be able to cope.

Thus recorded crime can only be seen as an indication of criminal activity. One Chief Constable has estimated that only about 10 per cent of all crime is reported to the police. As you might expect, a much higher proportion of serious crime is liable to be reported to the police and thus recorded. The reporting rate, and the detection rate, for murder is over 90 per cent, and for serious assault over 80 per cent. Such crimes are, by their very nature, difficult to hide, and they are crimes to which the police will devote great effort and resources to solve and 'clear up'. In contrast, petty theft has a very low rate of reporting to the police, and a low detection rate. Therefore, the degree to which official statistics underestimate the actual level of crime depends on the particular category of crime. Almost all cars that are stolen are reported for the simple reason that that is the only way owners will get insurance compensation; and insurance is often a major reason for reporting other thefts and burglary. So the extension of insurance provision has led to a greater likelihood of the reporting of many crimes.

There are a number of reasons why crimes are not reported to the police and thus not recorded in the official criminal statistics. Below we will suggest and discuss some of these reasons. Before reading through these suggestions you might like to jot down some of your own ideas, or to discuss possible explanations with colleagues. This list is by no means exhaustive and is only intended to illustrate some of the most commonplace reasons for the non-reporting of crime.

Firstly, many crimes do not have victims, and only the offender(s) will know that a crime has been committed – for example, illegal drug use and supply, soliciting by prostitutes or illegal abortion (here we are talking about victims in the conventional sense of a separate and visible victim, although it could be argued that the user of illegal drugs is a victim him or herself, or that the unborn foetus is a victim in the case of illegal abortion). These 'victimless' crimes often involve one party or individual providing a service which the other party wants. In the examples given above neither of the parties involved would inform the police; consequently the true numbers of such crimes are never known to the police. The extent to which these crimes are known and recorded will depend almost entirely on police activity and efficiency.

Secondly, embarrassment may be a reason for not reporting a crime; victims may want to hide an offence rather than report it. This is particularly the case with victims of sexual offences. Rape victims, for example, may fear the consequences of reporting the act, and may not wish to be cross-examined by the police or in court and be exposed to possible innuendoes and suggestions that they 'encouraged' their assailant. Recent court cases where the victims of rape have been seen by judges as contributing to the crime through their 'negligence' – for example hitch-hiking alone – are not likely to act as an encouragement for other victims to report such offences. Thus, very serious crimes might go unrecorded. Similarly, parents of children who have been victims of sexual offences may not want their child to be interrogated and to go through the trauma of reliving the experience in court.

Thirdly, and linked with the above point, it is sometimes not in the best interest of the victim to report a crime to the police. Firms may not wish to prosecute an employee who has been fiddling them but may prefer to deal with the matter informally, to avoid bad publicity or appearing inefficient and the possible loss of the confidence of their clients.

Fourthly, victims may feel that there is no point in informing the police, because there is no chance of getting retribution. Minor thefts, for example, may not be reported as the victims feel there is little chance of them getting their goods back or of the offender getting caught.

Fifthly, victims or witnesses of crimes may dislike or not trust the police. Crimes among criminals are not likely to be reported to the police for obvious reasons. In a similar vein, victims or witnesses may sympathise with the offender, or be unwilling to inform on a member of their family or a friend.

Another reason for the non-reporting of crime is that many victims are unaware that they actually are victims of specific crimes. Firms may be unaware of theft by their employees, and shops will not be aware of particular instances of shoplifting. Such actions are commonly built into firms' and shops' accounting procedures, as 'stock shrinkage' perhaps.

Thus, an unknown but potentially vast amount of crime remains unknown to the police, and is therefore not included in official criminal statistics. Furthermore, even when examining recorded crimes only, changes in the figures may be accounted for by reasons other than the fact that the actual number of offences have changed, and there are a variety of other ways in which an increase in recorded crime can be accounted for. Below we will suggest and examine a number of possible reasons or explanations. Again, our list is not intended to be exhaustive and you might try to suggest other potential reasons.

Firstly, improved police efficiency will affect the rate of recorded crime. Better police equipment might lead to more offences being recorded, as might an increase in police numbers, and over the last few years there has been a recruitment drive by the police.

Secondly, and linked with this point, criminal statistics reflect the intensity of law enforcement itself. The police may respond to pressure to concentrate their time and resources on certain specific areas of criminal activity, often areas which have received heavy coverage in the mass media, such as football hooliganism or drug use. In such circumstances the figures for those activities will rise as a result of the police having spent more time and money in dealing with them.

Thirdly, an increased willingness on the part of the public to report offences will influence the statistics. There may, for example, be changes in public opinion towards the police and the reporting of criminal activity. It is also relevant to add that it has become increasingly easy to report matters to the police as a result of the spread of private telephones.

A fourth and very important influence on the rate of recorded crime is the effect of changes in the law, which may lead to an alteration in the definition of what is or is not a crime. In general terms, there are far more laws in operation today than in the past, thus there are more laws to be broken. So legal changes, not merely changes in behaviour, will be reflected in the statistics. On this point, a central problem with criminal statistics is that they only cover what is officially defined as crime at any one time. Thus new definitions of crime and new laws raise problems in the comparison of statistics on a 'before and after' basis, and thereby lead to problems in talking about rises or falls in crime.

Fifthly, there are greater opportunities for crime in modern society. For example, the huge increase in the number of motor vehicles has led to a massive increase in auto-crimes. The growth of self-service stores since the Second World War has been important in encouraging shoplifting. It is likely that certain crimes have increased not because people have become more dishonest but because it has become easier to commit such crimes. Similarly, the much greater availability of illegal drugs has led to a phenomenal growth in drug offences.

A final possible reason – which relates to police practice – is that individual police officers may feel under pressure to make arrests in order to appear efficient and to get on. As a young policewoman interviewed as part of a recent study on Merseyside's police said, 'It's always at the back of your mind, you just can't get rid of it. Oh hell, I've got to do somebody. I've got my progress (report) due'. (**McClure, J.**, *Spike Island*, **1981**).

So the more closely one looks at the criminal statistics the more complicated and problematic they become. And the more dubious must we be of sweeping generalisations made on the basis of such statistics. It may be that we are becoming a more 'criminal' nation as the increase in crime rates would suggest, but this cannot just be assumed and it is important to be aware of other possible reasons for such an increase. At the same time it is obvious that full enforcement of the law would be totally impractical. The police have to exert some *discretion*. If the police recorded and acted on every offence they knew about, they would be overwhelmed with paperwork and the courts would be flooded with cases. The police officer on patrol has to ask whether it is worth proceeding with and against every suspect, and will often decide it is not worth it. One of the arguments we will examine below is the view that the police use this discretion, this freedom to decide when to proceed and when not to, to favour 'respectable' and middle-class individuals rather than working-class individuals.

The middle-class bias in statistics

As well as questioning the validity and use of official criminal statistics, more fundamental questions as to their meaning and implications have also been raised. There is no doubt for one thing, that these statistics are incomplete. In developing theories of crime this would not necessarily be important if the figures gave a representative sample of crime and criminals. For example, if only 10 per cent of crime is recorded in the statistics, but this nevertheless accurately reflects the full range of crime and criminals, then the statistics would provide a representative sample. However, it has been demonstrated that the official criminal statistics give an unrepresentative and misleading picture of the social distribution of criminal behaviour.

Recent studies of crime, particularly Marxist-based work, have suggested that there is a systematic bias in favour of the powerful in the way that the law is applied and enforced. Broadly speaking, the higher an individual is in the social strata the less likely he or she is to be arrested, prosecuted and (if prosecuted) found guilty. Of course, this is not the same as saying that the rich and powerful never get prosecuted: there are many specific cases which illustrate this point, and which are generally well publicised. Nonetheless, such instances tend to be exceptions to the rule.

The statistics show that recorded crime is predominantly working-class. To assess whether this is an accurate picture it is necessary to address the question as to whether crime itself is predominantly working-class. The issue to examine is whether the fact that more working-class offenders are caught means that more working-class people break laws. A number of factors need to be taken into account here, and we will examine some of them below.

Those crimes which are reported are more likely to be committed by the working class because they are more visible, such as crimes against property. Middle-class crimes, such as fraud or embezzlement, are far less likely to be discovered and reported. Furthermore, people are more likely to report suspicious circumstances surrounding an individual who appears to be of lower-class origin.

Whether intentionally or not, police procedures may be biased against those of lower social status. When a crime is reported to the police they do not work on the assumption that anyone could have done it. This is not practical or possible. Therefore, they tend to look for a certain 'type'. This is a very important factor because it biases police activity against the poorly spoken, badly dressed and ill-educated individuals who have the least power, and the fewest people of influence to back them up.

There is also an element of bias when the individual comes into contact with the official, whether police officer or magistrate, which has similarities with the relationship between middle-class teachers and working-class pupils. The police tend to operate with different expectations of individuals from different social backgrounds. They are far more likely to use their discretion when dealing with the middle-class offender, thus the middle-class offender is far less likely to actually come to court. It is important to bear in mind that there may be a significant amount of delinquency and crime amongst the middle classes, but we are less likely to be made aware of it. 'One law for the rich and another for the poor' is an old saying which is certainly true of the way the law is enforced. To provide an illustration, a child who gets into trouble is much more likely to come before a court if he or she is from a poor home and has parents who do not get on with the welfare authorities or the police, than if his or her family is prosperous, respectable and willing to co-operate with the police and social services.

In the last section of this chapter we will examine the attempts that have been made to find out more about the actual extent of crime, and to provide some sort of indication of the 'dark figure' of crime and to discover the 'real' rather than the recorded rate and character of crime. The two major forms such attempts have taken are victim studies and self-report studies.

Victim studies and self-report studies

While victim studies and self-report studies overlap to some extent and are sometimes used in conjunction, they are distinct approaches which need to be defined separately.

Victim or victimisation studies are designed to investigate the number of individuals who have been victims of crime. They 'took off' in the mid-1960s in the USA. A Washington survey, for example, showed that 38 per cent of those asked revealed that they had been a victim of a serious crime within the last year, compared to the 10 per cent revealed by police statistics. The purpose of this and of other victim studies was to elicit from respondents whether they had been the victim of a crime, and if so, which types of crime and whether they had reported it to the police.

All victim studies show that police records cover, at the most, about one quarter of the serious crime actually committed. Such studies do themselves, however, suffer from limitations. For example, individuals find it difficult to remember how often they have been 'victimised', or tend to exaggerate their experiences. Moreover, while they do show that official statistics tend to underestimate the amount of crime, it is likely that victim studies also under-record the amount – mostly because people can only report having been victims of crime if they know that they have been victimised. Although such a statement is transparently obvious, as we have demonstrated earlier there are a vast number of crimes where people do not know they are victims, such as minor thefts, and many white-collar crimes.

Nonetheless, it is likely that victim studies provide a fairly reliable guide for measuring 'conventional' crimes such as assault, robbery and burglary, where the individual will be well aware that he or she was victim. Even with such 'conventional' crimes, however, different people might interpret events differently, and there might be a degree of under-reporting because of this. Some people may define a vague tampering with a door or window at night as an 'attempted burglary' while others will not.

Victim's interpretations and memories indicate that victim studies cannot be assumed to accurately reflect the 'real' extent of crime; and the search for more reliable and direct indicators has included the development of self-report studies.

Self-report studies usually involve asking people to give information about their past illegal activities, in response to a questionnaire or interview. As well as being asked how often they commit illegal acts, respondents are generally asked details of their social characteristics, social class, race and so on, in an attempt to get round the biases in official criminal statistics.

A range of self-report studies have indicated that a majority of people admit to some kind of illegal activity, whether trivial or serious, which could result in a court appearance. For example, studies have shown that 90 per cent of boys in the Inner London area admit to having travelled on public transport without a ticket, or to deliberately under-paying; 82 per cent admit breaking windows of empty houses; and only a small percentage claim to have committed no offences.

Again, there are likely to be problems of reliability with such data. Will people admit to having committed criminal offences, even if they are guaranteed confidentiality? It seems to go against common-sense notions that individuals would want to hide any misdemeanours or crimes. Alternatively, respondents may exaggerate their delinquencies out of bravado, especially likely with juveniles. Others may under-report due to dishonesty, forgetfulness or paranoia. Attemps that have been made to check the 'honesty' of respondents have indicated that about a quarter of respondents are liable to conceal information.

A further difficulty is the impossibility of including all criminal acts in a questionnaire or interview. Thus, the researcher has to be selective, which raises problems as to which offences should be mentioned and questioned about and which not. As you will realise, some offences are predominantly working-class and others predominantly middle-class, and it is important that self-report studies do not include too many offences typical of one group or class.

A final problem with self-report studies concerns the representativeness of the sample being studied. Many self-report studies have been carried out in schools, which will tend to result in school drop-outs and truants being excluded from the sample and lead to an unrepresentative sample. Also, those most likely not to complete the questionnaire or do the interview are most likely to be delinquent; and one cannot force people to fill in questionnaires correctly.

Notwithstanding these difficulties, self-report studies do indicate that middle-class individuals are as likely to commit crimes as working-class individuals.

The British Crime Sruvey of 1983, a research project carried out by the Home Office, is a recent example of how victim and self-report studies can be used to attempt to get round the problems of and deficiences with the official criminal statistics.

The first report was written by **Mike Hough and Pat Mayhew** and involved in-depth interviews with 11,000 households in England and Wales. People were asked what crimes they had been victims of (victim study) and about their own law-breaking (self-report study), and they were also asked about their attitudes towards the police and policing. Thus, this survey combined the two methods we have been looking at above.

While such victim and self-report surveys are not new what was new for this country was the scope of this survey. The *British Crime Survey* showed that there were about four times as many crimes committed each year as the police were ever told about. Although such figures might create public alarm, the main reason given for non-reporting was because the offence was considered too trivial to waste police time (38 per cent of reasons given), or that the police could do nothing about it (16 per cent). Fear or dislike of the police was way down the list, at 6 per cent. The survey also found that those who most feared violence, the elderly and women, were the least likely to experience it, while those most at risk were young males who went out regularly. With regard to particular crimes, the survey perhaps offered some reassurance to those accustomed to the image of a massive upsurge in crime which is so regularly portrayed by the media. The average household can expect to be burgled once every forty years, for example, while violent confrontation between the intruder and victim is very rare – one per cent of all cases. The survey tells us that the chances of being burgled are less than the risk of domestic fire and that the chances of robbery are smaller than those of being admitted to a psychiatric hospital – not that such statistics will be a lot of consolation to those who are burgled or robbed.

The *British Crime Survey* suggests that one in four crimes are officially reported, although sociologists and criminologists suggest that between 10 and 15 per cent is a more probable figure. However, such a difference can be reconciled, because these type of victim-based surveys can only include crimes where there is a victim who can be interviewed. Thus, they exclude a range of offences, such as shoplifting and stealing from work, where the non-reporting is particularly high. Furthermore, some interviewees will not wish to talk about painful experiences just for the benefit of a survey interviewer.

The figure of one in four crimes being reported refers to crime in general, and this ratio of recorded to unrecorded crime varies according to the particular crime. The survey shows that there were twice as many burglaries as were recorded by the police, nearly five times as much wounding, twelve times as much theft from the person and, most unexpectedly perhaps, thirteen times as much vandalism or criminal damage to personal and household property. Thus, the 'dark figure' of unrecorded crime depends on the sort of offences that are considered, and if different groups of offence categories are examined, different ratios will be found.

To conclude our review of criminal statistics, it is clear that official statistics on crime, like most statistics, should not be taken at face value as 'facts' to be accepted uncritically. They are the product of social processes and they involve the activities not just of offenders but also of decision-makers and enforcers in the area of law and order. Attempts to remedy the deficiencies in these statistics suffer from a number of problems and difficulties themselves. In fact, any crime rate, whether produced by the police, victim study, self-report study or whatever, will depend on a classification of crime that is socially produced.

5 Documentary readings

The purpose of this chapter is to fill out certain of the areas of the study of crime which have been discussed or referred to in earlier chapters, and to provide readings or extracts from original sociological work in this field. Some of the extracts are extended illustrations of particular areas and issues in the study of crime; others illustrate particular theoretical or methodological issues. Extracts from a number of the studies referred to in the previous chapters are included; as are extracts from works not specifically cited in these chapters but which are closely related to topics and issues raised in them.

As far as possible, the extracts are ordered so as to follow the structure of the earlier chapters. Thus, extracts related to Chapter 2 precede those related to Chapter 3 and so on, although certain studies are of course relevant to more than one particular aspect of the sociology of crime. Each of the extracts is introduced briefly and related and cross-referenced to earlier section(s) of the book.

H. S. Becker: Problems in the study of crime and deviance

In his famous study, *Outsiders*, Becker outlines the basic interactionist approach to the study of crime and deviance. It has become one of the basic and seminal texts in the sociological study of this topic. The first two chapters explain the labelling perspective, with later chapters applying this perspective to specific types of deviant behaviour, such as drug use. In the final chapter Becker discusses some of the problems involved in the study of crime and deviance. The following extract is taken from this last chapter, and elaborates on some of the problems we mentioned in our first chapter, (pp 7–8).

Reading 1

It is in the nature of the phenomenon of deviance that it will be difficult for anyone to study both sides of the process and accurately capture the perspectives of both classes of participants, rule-breakers and rule-enforcers. Not that it is impossible, but practical considerations of gaining access to situations and the confidence of the people involved in any reasonable length of time mean that one will probably study the situation from one side or the other. Whichever class of participants we choose to study and whose viewpoint we therefore choose to take, we will probably be accused of 'bias'. It will be said that we are not doing justice to the viewpoint of the opposing group. In presenting the rationalisations and justifications a group offers for doing things as it does, we will seem to be accepting its rationalisations and justifications and accusing other parties to the transaction in the words of their opponents. If we study drug addicts, they will surely tell us and we will be bound to report that they believe the outsiders who judge them are wrong and inspired by low motives. If we point to those aspects of the addict's experience which seem to him to confirm his beliefs, we will seem to be making an apology for the addict. On the other hand, if we view the phenomenon of addiction from the point of view of the enforcement officials, they will tell us and we will be bound to report that they believe addicts are criminal types, have distrubed personalities, have no morals and cannot be trusted. We will be able to point to those aspects of the enforcer's experiences which justify their view. In so doing, we will seem to be agreeing with his view. In either case, we shall be accused of presenting a one-sided and distorted view.

But this is not really the case. What we are presenting is not a distorted view of 'reality', but the reality which engages the people we have studied, the reality they create by their interpretation of their experience and in terms of which they act. If we fail to present this reality, we will not have achieved full sociological understanding of the phenomenon we seek to explain.

Becker, H. S., *Outsiders: studies in the sociology of deviance,*
1963, pp. 173–174

Discussion question

1 Sociological research into crime faces particular problems due to the nature of the subject being investigated. Suggest some of these problems.

A. K. Cohen: The delinquent subculture

In the first chapter of his study, *Delinquent Boys*, Cohen provides a very clear definition of the term delinquent subculture, with the main portion of the book then showing how this subculture is vital to the occurrence of delinquency. Below we reproduce Cohen's definition of a delinquent subculture.

Reading 2

The expression, 'the delinquent subculture', may be new to some readers of this volume. The idea for which it stands, however, is a commonplace of folk – as well as scientific – thinking. When Mrs Jones says: 'My Johnny is really a good boy but got to running around with the wrong bunch and got into trouble', she is making a set of assumptions which, when spelled out more explicitly, constitute the foundations of an important school of thought in the scientific study of juvenile delinquency. She is affirming that delinquency is either an inborn disposition nor something the child has contrived by himself; that children learn to become delinquents by becoming members of groups in which delinquent conduct is already established and the 'thing to do'; and that a child need not be 'different' from other children, that he need not have any twists or defects of personality or intelligence, in order to become a delinquent.

In the language of contemporary sociology, she is saying that juvenile delinquency is a subculture. . .

When we speak of a delinquent subculture, we speak of a way of life that has somehow become traditional among certain groups in American society. These groups are the boys' gangs that flourish most conspicuously in the 'delinquent neighbourhoods' of our large American cities. The members of these gangs grow up, some to become law-abiding citizens and others to graduate to more professional and adult forms of criminality, but the delinquent tradition is kept alive be the age-groups that succeed them. . .

Delinquency, according to this view, is not an expression or contrivance of a particular kind of personality; it may be imposed upon any kind of personality if circumstances favour intimate association with delinquent models. The process of becoming a delinquent is the same as the process of becoming, let us say, a Boy Scout. The difference lies only in the cultural pattern with which the children associates.

> Cohen, A. K., *Delinquent Boys: the culture of the gang,*
> 1955, pp. 11–14

Discussion questions

1 In what ways does the social environment predispose certain individuals to join delinquent subcultures?
2 Discuss some of the difficulties with the concept of the delinquent subculture (refer to the section on subcultural theories in Chapter 2).

G. Pearson: The history of crime and delinquency

In Chapter 3, we examined in some detail Pearson's review of the history of street crime in Britain, and his criticism of the widely held belief that such crime is a unique feature of present-day society. The following extract from this fascinating historical study deals with the problems of locating a 'golden age' when Britain was relatively free of crime and lawlessness.

Reading 3

Now, what I wish to ask in this book is whether this way of thinking about Britain's decline is useful and accurate. And if it is not (and I will argue that it is not) then to what extent does this tradition of anguished regret for the past hinder our actions in the present and the future?. . .

This view of Britain's history as one founded on stability and decency is deeply ingrained in the self-understanding of the British people. The present, we hardly need to be told, is extremely tense. But the past, say the accumulated traditions of our national culture, was a 'golden age' of order and security. Nowadays we need the iron fist of policing in order that we might sleep soundly in our beds. Whereas formerly we did not, and our love of tolerant freedom was spontaneous, unregimented and natural.

The extremity of these awful judgements against the moral deterioration of the British people, and the enormous vision of chaos and disorder which they conjure up, suggest the need for a cautious organisation of our thought and feeling as we approach these matters. Clearly, there is an impressive consistency in this line of thinking – both in terms of the belief in a pre-existing era of tranquility, and in the agreement that the natural moderacy of the 'British way of life' has been eclipsed in the hooligan deluge. However, when we come to more details considerations – such as exactly where this 'golden age' is to be located in real historical time – then we are confronted with such a disorderly jumble of datemarks and vague historical allusions as to allow for wide margins of disagreement even among dedicated 'law-and-order' enthusiasts. Indeed, at the centre of the preoccupation with declining standards and mounting disorder, there is an immense historical 'black hole'.

Pearson, G., *Hooligan: A history of respectable fears,*
1983, pp. 7–8

P. Corrigan: Contemporary delinquency – the problem of leisure

In our discussion of delinquency in contemporary society (Chapter 3, pp. 34–35) we looked at Paul Corrigan's study of working-class boys in the north-east of England. Corrigan points out that the delinquency of these boys cannot be explained or understood outside the context of their leisure activities (or lack of them). In particular, the boys drift into and out of minor delinquencies while hanging around the streets in groups looking for something to do, as the following extract from his study illustrates.

Reading 4

It was between the area of talking, joking and carrying on that things emerged that the boys called 'ideas'. These 'ideas'

formed the basis for group action and it is the way in which
these spontaneously evolve and are carried out that constitutes
one of the most active elements of 'hanging about'. . .

Albert (one of the boys studied): Well, somebody gets a
weird idea into their head, and they start to carry it out, and
others join in.

Question: Weird idea?

Albert: Things. . .like going around smashing milk bottles.

Boys on a Saturday night in Sunderland, in a group, on a
street corner, are aware that they are 'doing nothing' and are
bored with it in their own minds, essentially wanting something to happen. They want to have an interesting or exciting
time, a time that would not be boring, where they could create
some action. . .

If we analyse the street-corner activity of doing nothing in
groups in the light of always hoping that something will
happen, then the creation and the putting into effect of 'ideas'
by the group can be seen as one of the most significant group
experiences. Their significance is not only in terms of the
group experience but also in terms of the wider society, for it
is these ideas born out of the street-corner groups, doing
nothing, that are to a large extent the 'juvenile delinquency' of
the police and criminologists. Most significantly, these ideas
are born out of boredom and the expectation of future and
continuing boredom, and this affects the sort of ideas that they
are. A good 'idea' must contain the seeds of continuing change
(from the boring situation) as well as excitement and involvement. Smashing milk bottles is a good example of this since it
typifies the way in which they are put into effect. Methodolo-
gically, it is not possible for any researcher to get the kids to
talk with much sense of ideas since the question 'Why?' to the
smashing of milk bottles is one that is not possible for the boy
to answer outside the context of the whole Saturday evening. . .

For the sort of interaction that we are referring to here is not
the *planned* smashing of things. It is not that boys go out on a
Saturday night looking for milk bottles or other things to
smash. Rather they use smashing as something interesting to
do. . .

Question: What sort of things do you do on a Saturday
evening?

Peter: Usually play football down the street, play footy. Just gang down the court or somewhere then come home.

Question: What other things do you do?

Peter: On Saturday I knock around with me mates.

Question: What do you do?

Peter: Well, cause trouble, you know; play knocking on doors, throw stones at windows and that. Cause fights mostly.

Is is *really* necessary to explain the excitement of smashing things, whether they are milk bottles, shop windows, buses, telephone boxes or whatever, if the alternative is to stand there and do nothing.

Corrigan, P., *Schooling the Smash Street Kids,* 1979, pp. 128–130

Discussion questions

1 Which sociological method do you feel would be most appropriate to the sort of research carried out by Corrigan?
2 Suggest possible difficulties with the use of other sociological methods for studying the leisure activities of these boys.
3 Explain how boredom is crucial to the sort of minor delinquencies Corrigan is examining.

M. Levi: The corporate criminal in prison

In Chapter 3 we looked at Levi's study of long-firm fraud as an example of corporate crime. Below we include a brief extract from this study which looks at the problems and consequences of conviction for the business, 'respectable' criminal in comparison to the regular criminal – bearing in mind, of course, that the business criminal is far less likely to be convicted that most other types of criminal.

Reading 5

Most long-firm fraudsters manage quite successfully in prison, although its entertainments and amenities are hardly to their taste. . . They are rarely troublesome prisoners, although they often continue their 'operator' habits while inside. . . Long-firmers are experienced manipulators, and they make entertaining company for both prisoners and staff. Consequently, unless there are 'gangsters' around, they usually manage to get the best jobs in prison. . .

It might be argued that despite their relative success at 'making out' in prison, long-firm fraudsters suffer far greater 'relative deprivation' than do other prisoners. For on the outside, they live far more lavishly than do 'ordinary' criminals, and experience a correspondingly greater contrast between 'normal' and prison life. . . Although there is some truth in this relative deprivation argument, it is equally important to note that the pains of imprisonment are mitigated by pleasant recollections: to be doing 'a lot of bird' without having lived well seems far more futile and absurd that to be paying for the rich fruits that crime has already brought. At least there are benefits to be weighed against the costs!

Levi, M., *The Phantom Capitalists: the organisation and control of long-firm fraud*, 1981, pp. 115–116

Discussion question

1 Why might sentencers – judges and magistrates – treat middle-class, business criminals more leniently than those convicted of more 'conventional' crimes?

G. Mars: Cheats at work: employee theft

In Chapter 3 we discussed briefly employee theft, and, in particular, Ditton's study of fiddling at a factory-production bakery. In a similar vein, Mars has studied the everyday crimes of normal people in the normal circumstances of their work – what Ditton calls 'part-time crime'. Mars is not concerned with the spectacular or the 'one-off' crime, but with activities that are an accepted part of everyday jobs. The extent and variety of these activities are astonishing, but while almost everyone is aware of them, and although the majority of us fiddle in one way or another, fiddling is generally considered a trivial activity without serious implications. Mars' book challenges this view, and we will include two extracts from it. The following extract is part of an examination of how management have periodic 'purges' on their workforce in an attempt to control and crack down on fiddling.

Reading 6

When workers think a periodic purge is imminent, everyone feels equally threatened. No one knows where lightening may strike, the precise purpose of an investigation, or who specifically will be investigated. So everyone takes avoiding action. A waitress told me of such an incident when she heard a rumour that her hotel management had appointed private detectives with the power to search staff homes – a not uncommon fear among hotel workers and one paralleling similar periodic fears in other occupations of this type.

I was at the Embassy then, and it used to be very busy. Everyone was fiddling like mad when we got a leak through from the office that they were sending private detectives round the houses. . .I was petrified because all my sheets and tableclothes and all my cutlery and silver were all stamped with the Embassy crest. Well, I didn't know that to do. As I say, I was petrified! So I made an excuse, I said I was ill, and rushed off home. I piled everything I could on a sheet in the middle of the floor and tied up the corners. . .I dashed into the garden – out there – and started digging a bloody great hole. I wasn't laughing at the time, though, I can tell you, because the more I dug down, the more I was digging up! There was a pile of coffee pots, cutlery and rotten linen already in the garden that had been buried there by the waiter who'd had the house before me! He must have done exactly the same thing as I did when the panic hit him.

Mars, G., *Cheats at Work: an anthropology of workplace crime*, 1982, pp. 130–131

Later in the book, Mars attempts to put fiddles into context, to point out the conditions that favour them and the places where they are most likely to flourish. The opportunities and indeed the pressures for people to fiddle vary widely and Mars suggests a number of 'fiddle-prone' factors attached to particular occupations. One of these factors he terms 'exploiting expertise', and is the subject of our second extract.

Reading 7

A widespread factor is found where real or suggested expertise is involved in a transaction and where at the same time it may be assumed that the customer is ignorant about what it is he is paying for. This factor therefore depends upon an imbalance in power which is based on an imbalance in knowledge.

These conditions *typically* exist in garage servicing, though they are by no means confined to it. They are indeed well represented among repairmen of all kinds and are also found, to a degree, among the professions. It is useful, however, if we begin this discussion with garage servicing. . .

The economic base to garage servicing (following O'Brien, *Motor magazine*, 10th September 1977) lacks two conditions that normally operate in pricing: the first is that consumers should have speedy knowledge of defects in what they buy; the second that they are free to move from an unsatisfactory supplier to a more satisfactory one. In competitive trading these conditions exist and the price system benefits the consumer. . .

These two conditions are absent from garage servicing. O'Brien uses the phrase 'perverse incentives' to explain how a garage that performs poorly is likely to do better than one that performs well. He argues that bad garages drive out good ones because the typical customer cannot judge whether a service has been done properly, and it is difficult for him to check. Thus a garage can, with impunity, charge for a full service which has only been half done. . .

> For if a garage habitually does half the service its costs are very much lower than if it has done the full service; and since it can charge the full price, because of the ignorance of the consumer, its profits are maximised when it does as little of the service as it can get away with. There is probably some lower limit below which the garage will not go in skimping the service, because the risk of detection then becomes too high (O'Brien).

The garage benefits even further since faults from defective service are unlikely to occur immediately after collection of a vehicle. An ignorant motorist is likely, therefore, to absolve the garage from responsibility and pay it further to rectify these new faults.

Mars, G., *Cheats at Work: an anthropology of workplace crime*, 1982, pp. 142–144

Discussion questions

1 Suggest other situations where there is scope for 'fiddling' based on the superior knowledge of the provider of a service over the customer.
2 Another 'fiddle-prone' factor attached to certain occupations suggested by Mars is 'passing trade', where two sides of a transaction meet only once. How might 'passing trade' aid or encourage workplace crime?

A. Campbell: Shoplifting – the 'typical' female crime

This reading shows Anne Campbell's attempt to explain the relatively high involvement of females in shoplifting, sometimes seen as the 'typical' female crime. Contrary to popular belief, shoplifting is neither a new word nor a new occurrence. However, while shoplifting occurred in the past, the extent of the crime has grown massively in recent years. From 1939 to 1964, offences quadrupled to over 60,000 known offences. By 1972, that figure had doubled to over 120,000 offences and since then there has been a steady increase. Although popularly thought of as a female offence, women do not outnumber men among those found guilty. Over the last twenty years, women have made up just under 50 per cent of all convicted shoplifters. This still makes it the one serious, widespread offence in which the rate of female offenders is nearly equivalent to the rate of male offenders, as the table on page 49 illustrates.

Campbell suggests that there are extra pressures on girls which push them towards certain types of crime. Girls are brought up with calls to buy cosmetics, jewellery and clothes and to do what they can to enhance their looks. Thus, females tend to be more susceptible to the pressures of the market and the forces of consumerism than males. This will tend to incline them toward petty theft. Campbell focuses on girl shoplifters, but it should be stressed that other females who shoplift, perhaps pensioners or single parents, might do so for more basic material needs.

Reading 8

Studies of shoplifting have in the main concentrated either on the pathological individual personality of the offender or the shop policy that promotes this kind of behaviour. Very few studies have sought to position shoplifting within a broader social and political sphere, where women in particular are vulnerable to a consumer fetishism that drives them to law-breaking. . .

Girls, of course, are a particularly fruitful market. Even with subcultures, it is characteristically the females who are the most susceptible to fashion and cosmetic selling. As a group, women have historically been preoccupied with appearance-. . .(which) is capitalised upon by the fashion and beauty manufacturers, whose methods can be seen in any women's magazine. . .The common theme is the necessity of spending money to look good, and since fashions change, that requires a never-ending outlay of cash. . .

Why is (shoplifting) a crime in which girls participate in greater numbers than in any other offence? The answer given by many writers is solely in terms of the greater exposure among women to goods and shops: the simple opportunity thesis. But as well as this, it is important to consider the extent to which self-representation and appearance are particularly important to girls economically and therefore psychological-ly. . .

The message is clear: men want beauty not brains. The function of women is decorative. Every minute spent in physical self-improvement is an investment, not only material-ly but in terms of emotional adjustment too. To be old and unmarried still represents a cloud on a teenage girl's hori-zon. . .

Sharpe (*Just Like Girl*, 1976) looked at job preferences among a group of London girl school-leavers. Four girls in every 10 chose office work, and, by including the jobs of teachers, nurses, shop assistants, bank clerks, receptionists, telephonists, hairdressers and nannies, three-quarters of the choices were accounted for. . . With the exception of teaching and nursing, these jobs require little specialised training, and for most a good physical appearance is a distinct advantage. The importance of looks becomes even more pronounced when considering the types of occupations to which girls, often unrealistically, aspire – the glamour jobs. The role of air hostesses, models, actresses, public relations officers, sales

representatives, promotion girls and personal assistants is often one of sexual window–dressing and male ego-boosting.
Campbell, A., *Girl Delinquents*, 1981, pp. 117–131

Discussion questions

1 Discuss the extent to which females are judged by looks rather than ability. Examine some of the ways in which the media exerts pressures on females (and males) to look 'right'.
2 Campbell looks at the shoplifting of *young* females. What pressures might there be on *older* females, and males, to shoplift?

M. Cain: Different styles of policing and their effects on criminal statistics

Cain's study on rural and urban police forces illustrates very distinctly the differing styles of policing in different areas. It shows how these different styles are likely to have a marked effect on the crime statistics collected by particular police forces, an issue we looked at in the previous chapter on criminal statistics.

Reading 9

Certainly country policemen in the present study had a 'peace-keeping' orientation to their work. Their aim, explicitly, was to have a 'quiet patch'. . . A beat patrol was usually a leisurely affair, with ample time to stop and chat. People would address the beat policeman by name or else as 'sir', while he in turn would have a 'Good morning' for everyone encountered. . .

At the time of the study the city operated a system of foot patrols plus an emergency car service (distinct from traffic patrol). Two or three vehicles patrolled the division throughout the day, and it was claimed, with slight exaggeration, that any point could be reached within four minutes. . . The result was that the man left walking the beat had little of interest to do by way of responding to requests for emergency services. . . After postings to the cars and station offices this left 2⅔ men 'on the ground' per sub-division, or one man for every 26,838 of the population. Contrast this with the mean population of a rural one-man beat, a constant and stable 1,307 identifiable individuals. . .

There were three main responses by the men to this situation. The first, which was the officially approved response, was 'to make the work interesting' by developing contacts with shopkeepers and others on the beat, and keeping an eye open for unusual activity. . .

The second response to the endemic boredom, monotony and frequent cold, and to the impossibility of achieving the formally stated goals, was 'easing behaviour'. . .

The third means of making a dull and cold eight hours more tolerable was to seek marginally legitimate arrests. This gave excitement, the opportunity to go off duty early or at least to return to the warmth and relative conviviality of the police station, as well as prestige. . .

During 1963, at the central police station on the research division, 76 per cent of the 611 arrests made by uniformed men were for offences against the public order such as vagrancy, loitering, and above all drunkenness. . .

Impressions gained in this study suggest that 'crime work' ranks high in the police value system. . . Certainly men at the central station boasted proudly of the fact that they took more prisoners per year than any other division in the whole force.

Cain, M., 'On the Beat: interactions and relations in rural and urban police forces, in S. Cohen (ed.), *Images of Deviance*, 1971, pp. 66–74.

Discussion questions

1 What do you think Cain means by 'marginally legitimate arrests'? Suggest possible examples of such arrests.
2 How might criminal statistics (including both the extent of crime recorded and the character or type of crime) be influenced by the operation of the police rather than the amount of actual criminal behaviour?

G. Pearson: Problems with the historical study and comparison of crime

The main focus of our examination of criminal statistics, Chapter 4, was on the problems and deficiences with these statistics.

Pearson's study of the history of street cime in Britain clearly illustrates the problem of using criminal statistics as a means for comparing the rate of crime over extended periods of time. The following reading, from the final part of Pearson's book, gives specific examples of how changes in the way in which the law is enforced makes historical comparisons of the rate of criminality virtually impossible.

Reading 10

Criminal statistics are notoriously unreliable as measures of the actual extent of criminal activity, to such a degree that it is not unknown for historians to discount them altogether. The reason for their notoriety is that they are complicated by a number of factors others than real changes in the levels of crime. The growing size of the police force and its supporting apparatus is the most obvious and general factor. Changes in the routines of law enforcement, the increased mobility of the police, changes in what the law counts as crime, fluctuations in the vigour with which the law is applied, and shifts in public attitudes and tolerance – these must all be counted within the hidden dimensions of the manufacture of crime figures. . .

Between 1900 and the late 1970s. . . we are asked to strike comparisons between such different styles of law enforcement as to make little sense. First, in the earlier period there were wide margins of discretion within an extremely informal mode of policing – the proverbial clip around the ear, or the dreaded flick of the Edwardian policemen's rolled cape – which has been replaced by the more likely possibility of prosecution, or the issue of formal caution. And a formal caution, unlike a clip around the ear, goes into the record book as a 'known crime'. We have also seen how in earlier times people involved in acts of gross disorder would commonly be charged only with simple assault or drunkenness. . . street violence was too much of an everyday occurrence to count as 'real' crime. There was also a tendency not to record incidents which could not be cleared up. Until the 1930s, for example, it was a routine practice of the London police to record thefts reported to them by the public as 'lost property'. When this practice was changed, recorded levels of property crime soared: but, obviously, as a consequence of changes in policing and not as a result of changes in crime.

In overall terms, between 1900 and the present day, the state apparatus for collecting and sorting criminal information has changed so dramatically that we must question whether it can supply us with a valid measuring-stick with which to compare the two periods. The cluttered informality of the Edwardian local police station with its rudimentary procedures for record-keeping has been replaced by elaborate computer-assisted systems of information retrieval. And whether or not they enhance the efficiency of the police, they certainly expand the crime statistics. . . To ask us to strike meaningful comparisons across such a technological gulf is like trying to compare a theory of the origins of the universe based on observations through Galileo's lens with one facilitated by radio telescope. It simply will not do.

Pearson, G., Hooligan: A history of respectable fears,
1983, pp. 213–215

Discussion question

1 The first paragraph of this reading suggests a number of factors that will be reflected in the criminal statistics, aside from the actual rate of crime. The rest of the extract then examines how changes in the style of policing and law enforcement affect criminal statistics. Explain, with specific examples if possible, how the other factors referred to in the first paragraph (such as changes in what the law counts as crime, fluctuations in the vigour of the application of the law) determine or influence the criminal statistics.

D. J. Smith and J. Gray: The police and racial minorities

In Chapter 1 we made a distinction between informal and formal methods of social control. The former centre around the socialisation process, the way in which individuals learn and accept the values and norms of the wider society. The formal methods are based on the external and formal means for the enforcement of the law, and for the punishment of those who break the law. The following readings look at the main agent of law enforcement, the police. They are taken from the recent Policy Studies Institute (PSI) report on the Metropolitan Police force of London.

As with most areas of sociological study, it is not often that a simple and unproblematic definition can be established. And this is certainly the case with the distinction between formal and informal means of social control. The two overlap in many areas. While the police are clearly involved with formal social control, it is apparent that much of their work is carried out in an informal manner. Police work involves a considerable degree of flexibility and discretion.

In terms of their relations with the wider public, the police tend to be a particularly segregated group in society. Public opinion toward them varies from suspicion to hostility, and a major police problem would appear to be relations with the public. The PSI report indicates that roughly half of the London population have serious doubts about the standard of police conduct, although in most cases police misconduct was not seen as a normal, everyday occurrence. The PSI report is the most detailed study of a British police force yet produced, and Section Four of the report, entitled 'The police and people in London', examines the relationship between the police and the public in some depth.

In contrast to the image of police work as exciting and dangerous (an image which the police themselves tend to stress), patrolling was invariably boring and somewhat aimless, as the first of our extracts illustrates.

Reading 11

A considerable amount of police behaviour can best be understood as a search for some interest, excitment or sensation. An officer on foot will often spend a whole shift without doing any police work, and without talking to anyone except to greet them and provide simple information. . . Even officers in cars with mainsets can spend several hours without responding to a call and without finding something to do on their own account. Of course, there are times when a car rushes straight from one call to another one, but overall these are definitely unusual except in certain very restricted areas.

The importance of boredom and aimlessness is very much

obscured by most popular treatments of police work, whether in fictional or in documentary style. They naturally concentrate on the interesting bits, and, so, of course, do the police themselves. . .

Most constables would like to have a reasonable number of dramatic or at least interesting crimes to deal with. One PC complained at length to a sergeant that the 'ground' where they both worked had become much quieter; he looked back with nostalgia to the old days when the ground was much 'harder' and 'you could literally be strolling past a pub and a bloke would come staggering out with a knife in his back. . . '

A considerable number of stops are carried out mainly for something to do. When DJS (D. J. Smith) spent a whole night walking with a probationer who could find nothing at all to do, the probationer eventually waited on a main road where there was virtually no traffic and stopped the first two cars that came by. Both were young men on their way to work, and both said they were very frequently stopped by police at about 5 am as they went to work.

Smith D. J. and Gray, J., *Police and People in London: the police in action*, 1983, pp. 51–55

Discussion question

1 Aside from shift workers, which groups of people are disproportionately liable to be stopped and questioned by the police? Discuss how this might affect police relations with such groups.

One aspect of the attitudes and behaviour of the police which the report examined was with regard to race, and the police's relations with coloured people. Our second extract is taken from the section of the report which deals with the police and ethnic minorities.

Reading 12

Police officers often use racialist language (among themselves) for effect, but it is the more casual and automatic use of such language that is the most telling. . . racialist language is quite commonly used over the personal radio. For example, JG (J.

Gray) heard the inspector of the relief with which he was working say over the personal radio, 'Look, I've got a bunch of coons in sight'. The inspector was standing in a public place at the time, and of course this message came up over the radios of all police officers on the Division. . .

Although the terms by which police officers refer to black people are in common use in various other social contexts, they seem to be more commonly used within the Met than in most other groups: there can be few other groups in which it is normal, automatic, habitual to refer to black people as 'coons', 'niggers' and so on. . .

Police officers who expressed a racist ideology are certainly a small minority. Those who initiate racialist talk (without referring to a racist ideology) may be a minority too, but since they are rarely contradicted or opposed they tend to shape the norms of the group. A young probationer WPC put it like this.

'I know that PCs call them spooks, niggers and sooties, but deep down the majority of PCs aren't really against them, although there are some who really hate them and will go out of their way to get them. I call them niggers myself now, but I don't really mean it.'

This quotation gives a vivid insight into how someone who is basically sympathetic towards black people can come to adopt a racialist language in order to conform to the expectations of the group, which are set by a minority of active racists.

Smith D. J., and Gray, J., *Police and People in London: the police in action*, 1983, pp. 111–115.

Discussion questions

1 Discuss the effects of racialist language on coloured people's view of the police and the law.
2 Point to the links between racialist language of the police and the labelling process. How might this lead to the differential treatment of whites and blacks?
3 Should police officers be disciplined for using racialist language? (This issue could be developed into a more general consideration of whether police officers should be subject to more stringent codes or rules of behaviour than other people in society, given their position of authority).

References and further reading

Becker, H. S., *Outsiders: Studies in the Sociology of Deviance*, Free Press, New York, 1963.
> The classic statement on labelling and deviant behaviour. This study sets out the labelling theory, applies it to the study of marijuana users and dance musicians and looks at methodological problems in the study of crime and deviance.

Box, S., *Power, Crime and Mystification*, Tavistock, London, 1983.
> More specialised than his widely acclaimed *Deviance, Reality and Society* (Holt, Rinehart and Winston, London, 1981, second edition), this book focusses on a number of specific areas of the study of crime – including corporate crime, police crime, assaults on females and female crime.

Campbell, A., *Girl Delinquents*, Blackwell, London, 1981.
> Campbell examines whether female delinquency is substantially different from male delinquency, and looks at explanations for such behaviour in the family, educational and class background of female delinquents.

Cohen, S., (ed.) *Images of Deviance*, Penguin Books, Harmondsworth, 1971.
> Many of the articles in this collection have become widely quoted sources of information, such as Cain's work on the police, Taylor's on soccer hooliganism and Young's on the control of drug use. Cohen himself has become one of the seminal figures in the sociology of deviance in this country and his introduction to the book points to the need for the study of deviance to examine the making of rules and the control of rule-breaking as well as the deviant and criminal actions themselves.

Corrigan, P., *Schooling the Smash Street Kids*, Macmillan, London, 1979.
> A study of delinquency among boys based on research in Sunderland, Corrigan examines and criticises the notion of 'anti-school' subcultures.

Ditton, J., *Part-Time Crime: an ethnography of fiddling and pilferage*, Macmillan, London, 1977.
  Ditton provides a detailed description and analysis of fiddling at work based on his research in a medium-sized factory production bakery. The 'pressures' on employees to steal and not to 'rock and boat' are vividly illustrated.

Downes, D. and Rock, P., *Understanding Deviance: A guide to the sociology of crime and rule-breaking,* Clarendon Press, Oxford, 1982.
  A clear and thorough review of sociological theories of crime, including Functionalism, Subcultural theories, Interactionism, Control theories and Marxist theories.

Hough, M. and Mayhew, P., *The British Crime Survey: first report*, HMSO, 1983.
  This report is an overview of the findings of a national survey of crime in England and Wales which collected information about victimisation from a representative sample of 11,000 people. It looks at the extent of crime, the people most at risk, the fear of crime and people's experiences and expectations of the criminal justice system.

Levi M., *The Phantom Capitalists: the organisation and control of long-firm fraud*, Heinemann, London, 1981.
  Levi's study, which was discussed in Chapter 3, is a detailed examination of one type of fraud – long-firm fraud – which involves businesses running up large debts which they have no intention of paying. The research is based on interviews with fraudsters and with 'straight' businessmen, lawyers, judges, the police and other fraud investigators.

Mars, G., *Cheats at Work: an anthropology of workplace crime*, Allen and Unwin, London, 1982.
  An examination of workplace crime which covers a wide and diverse range of such activity. Mars points to the different nature and styles of 'fiddling'. In some occupations fiddles are carried out individually, in others there is group co-operation; in some there is collusion with management and in others such activity is quickly and severely punished.

Marsh, P., Rosser, E. and Harre, R., *The Rules of Disorder*, Routledge and Kegan Paul, London, 1978.
  This book looks at violence and disorder, particularly juvenile violence, through a study of the school classroom and football

grounds. The authors argue that juvenile delinquency tends to follow a ritualised pattern rather than being especially vicious in nature.

Pearson, G., *Hooligan: A history of respectable fears*, Macmillan, London, 1983.
Pearson's book gives the lie to the notion that hooliganism is a modern phenomenon. It is a journey back through the history of street crime in this country and the reactions to it from the press and 'respectable' society.

Smith, D. J. and Gray, J., *Police and People in London: the police in action*, Policy Studies Institute, London 1983.
This is a detailed report on the Metropolitan Police which looks at police norms and attitudes, police culture and the selection and training of police officers. Two readings from it are included in Chapter Five.

Taylor, I., Walton, P. and Young J., *The New Criminology*, Routledge and Kegan Paul, London, 1973.
After a comprehensive criticism of previous theories Taylor *et al.* outline and develop a Marxist, radical criminology. *Critical Criminology* (Routledge and Kegan Paul, London, 1975) is a selection of readings presenting different Marxist-based approaches and edited by the same authors.

Williams, J., Dunning, E. and Murphy, P., *Hooligans Abroad: behaviour and control of English fans at continental football matches*, Routledge and Kegan Paul, London, 1984.
A case study of English fans in Spain for the 1982 World Cup, and of English fans following club sides in Europe. Williams *et al.* illustrate the complexity of the phenomenon of football hooliganism and violence and the problems with simple causal explanations for such behaviour.

Index